A WORLD PORTRAIT OF GOLF

BRIAN MORGAN

**LIBRARY DISTRIBUTORS
OF
AMERICA**

31250 Cedar Valley Drive, Westlake Village, CA 91362

A WORLD PORTRAIT

OF GOLF

For Evangelyon

A special mention to my daughters Kirstie and Sharon
for all their patience.

Thanks to Dorothy, Kirstie and Doreen in my office;
to IGR in Japan for their help; to Ian Broadley for
his assistance and to all the clubs for allowing me
to photograph there. And to Nikon USA.

First published in 1988 in New York by Gallery
Books, an imprint of W.H. Smith Publishers Inc.,
112 Madison Avenue, New York, N.Y. 10016

ISBN 0-8317-9625-1

Title page illustration: St Andrews, Scotland

Designed by Neil H. Clitheroe
Typeset by Tradespools Ltd, Frome
Manufactured in Italy

CONTENTS

FOREWORD

Brian Morgan, in telling his story, has captured the diversity, the beauties, the humor of the global game of golf.

Inside you will find the joy, the fun, the very essence of what makes this game so special.

The Honors Course, whose primary purpose is to preserve and enhance amateur golf, takes great pride in bringing you this marvelous book – enjoy!

JOHN T. LUPTON
Chairman of the Board
The Honors Course

Opened in 1985, the Honors Course has quickly become one of America's most respected golf clubs. Owner John Lupton has dedicated the course to amateur golf and wants the members and guests to enjoy a unique facility. The Honors Course was designed by the famous golf architect, Pete Dye, who, even since the clubhouse opened, has returned regularly to supervise the final touches that go into making a good course great.

Like Augusta National, the Honors is an exclusive private members' club whose members mostly like to walk the course, assisted by caddies in splendid white uniforms. Driving out to the course from the nearby town of Chattanooga, the visitor could easily miss the entrance. A small sign and an unpretentious automatic gate are the only outward indications that the course exists. For golfers fortunate enough to pass through, an unforgettable experience awaits.

△ THE HONORS COURSE, TENNESSEE, USA
The par 3 8th hole. The uncultivated area between the tee and the green is strongly reminiscent of Scotland.

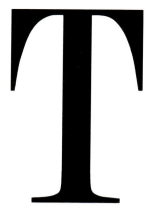

The title *A World Portrait of Golf* gives some clue to the contents, but my basic aim in putting this book together was to show in a picture-story format what it is like to play golf all over the world. I have tried to capture not merely the scenic splendour of some of the great championship courses, but also the particular 'atmosphere' of golf in each country; the customs and traditions that make golf, in many ways the simplest of all ball games, also one of the most entrancing.

The book has been slowly growing in my mind for several years now, but much of the photographic work was undertaken over a fifteen-month period, when I circled the globe no fewer than four times. During one particularly hectic spell at the beginning of 1987, I visited Tokyo three times, Australia, New Zealand, China, Hong Kong, Malaysia, Singapore and India – this in addition to such regular photographic duties as recording for posterity that annual rite of the golfing spring, the Masters Tournament, held each April in the beautiful setting of Augusta, Georgia.

Despite all the troubles and travails of international travel – lost baggage, missed connections, misunderstandings at airports – the international golf community remains a very close-knit and friendly one. As the late and much-lamented Henry Longhurst used to say, golf is the Esperanto of sport, a universal language that everyone can understand. It is indeed amazing how many people in different parts of the world know and communicate with each other because of a mutual love for the game. Although it would be impossible to thank individually all of those who have assisted with the preparation of this book, I must mention Mr Bhandari, an Indian member of the Royal and Ancient, whom I met totally by chance during the Masters at Augusta. As a result of his efforts, all the internal travel and accommodation arrangements for a tour of the Indian sub-continent were made and all the important people informed of my project, so that when I finally arrived I knew exactly where I was supposed to be at any one time – and more importantly so did everyone else! This made things infinitely easier.

There is an undeniable freemasonry in golf which was evident from South America to South Africa. Not so beyond the Iron Curtain. It was my intention to travel to Czechoslovakia, Yugoslavia, Romania and Bulgaria, but unhelpful officialdom, complications with visas and mind-boggling paperwork prevented this from being possible. India also presented a stopover problem. Arriving there *en route* from Katmandhu in Nepal, immigration officials in Calcutta revealed that I had marginally overstayed my 24-hour transit time and would have to return to Nepal. Scottish common sense eventually won the day and I was allowed to get on a flight to London. Meanwhile, political unrest in the aftermath of the Marcos régime prevented my intended visit to the Philippines.

In tropical climes, a photographer should never disregard the advice of the local help. Strange spiders, repellent reptiles and carnivorous beasts do not make for a steady hand. In the USA, and Arizona in particular, I make as much noise as is humanly possible to scare off the rattlers. You can never be too careful!

The weather is another insuperable adversary. I have lost count of the number of days I've wasted through inclement conditions while on location. The frustration of waiting, can, however, be compensated by capturing the unique freshness when, say, a storm has abated.

All golfers share certain preconceptions about the game as it is played in countries other than their own. Americans invariably think of British golf as a rather wild and windy pursuit, usually played by the sea. Conversely many Britons, conditioned by what they see on television and read in magazines, tend to expect all American courses to look as lush and beautifully manicured as Augusta in the spring.

I very much hope that this book will explode some of the myths and prejudices that still abound. Inevitably there are some gaps; I would have loved to include a picture from every country and island, no matter how remote, where golf is played, but that is perhaps a job for a future encyclopedia. What I have tried to include is a truly representative selection, showing every distinct facet of a game of quite extraordinary variety: given that my own collection of golfing slides now comes to well over half a million, choosing 220 for *A World Portrait of Golf* was no easy task. If, as a result of this book, just a few home-bound golfers are tempted to try some of the more exotic and far-flung courses of the world, then this whole project will have been worth while.

BRIAN MORGAN

Golf as we know it today started on our coastline where the natural linksland provided ideal, but tough, playing conditions.

Scotland has an abundance of public courses, from the majesty of St Andrews to the rugged difficulty of Carnoustie, both Open Championship venues, yet available for anyone to enjoy. I love the natural beauty of Scottish courses, with the heather, gorse, burns and lochs, combined with magnificent views and unlimited choice.

However, the biggest factor of golf in these islands is undoubtedly the weather. As a touring professional I can attest to that.

SAM TORRANCE

ST MELLION, CORNWALL, ENGLAND▷

GREAT BRITAIN AND IRELAND

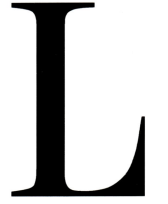

Learned speculation on the actual origins of the game could fill the shelves of several libraries, but there seems little doubt that what we now think of as golf existed in Scotland earlier than the seventeenth century. From the beginning a favoured location was the linksland, low-lying land between farmsteads and the sea, useful for grazing sheep but otherwise of little value. The sandy soil, undulating dunes and slow-growing grass were ideal for the nascent pastime, and in time distinct 'courses' evolved, each with varying numbers of holes depending upon the space available. To this day the premier championship of the world, the Open Championship, is still played on terrain that would have been easily recognizable to those early pioneers.

These simple, natural origins have meant that golf course architecture in Britain follows a distinct pattern, and perhaps the biggest difference of all between the home countries and the rest of the world lies in the budget for maintenance and upkeep. In the moderate British climate grass grows fairly slowly, hence it needs cutting less often, hence fewer staff are required; indeed in some of the smaller clubs no distinct full-time greenskeeper is employed at all, his duties being shared among the professional (if any) and such club members as are prepared to help with mowing, raking bunkers, and generally keeping things tidy.

One thing that will very quickly strike the American visitor to courses in Britain is the almost complete absence of motorized carts: these are often frowned upon, partly because of the damage they can do to the slow-growing turf, and partly because such carts are seen, perhaps perversely, as slowing down the game. Golf in Britain is played at a reasonably brisk pace, largely because of the climate. Anyone who has ever played at Sandwich or Brancaster in January, with a freezing gale blowing off the sea, will understand why the two and a half-hour foursome, rather than the five-hour fourball, is the favoured form of the game.

Another basic reason for the relative speed of golf in Britain is that it remains, in essence, a match-play game: outside defined medal competitions, very few male players keep their score in the fervent manner to which some of their American counterparts are accustomed, matching their cards for dollars and cents against their friends in the clubhouse afterwards. This may also perhaps explain why in Britain the back 'medal' tees are often small and rarely used – causing justifiable irritation to the overseas visitor who may have travelled thousands of miles to find a so-called 'championship course' truncated by up to a quarter of the nominal length on the scorecard.

Courses in Britain tend to be slightly shorter than their American counterparts, with the great majority measuring somewhere between 5750

and 6750 yards in all. In very dry spells this may appear a fairly moderate challenge, with the ball running seemingly for miles along hard, baked fairways, but once the wind and rain get up even fairly simple layouts can become positively tigerish. In many ways the weather is *the* single determining factor behind almost every distinctive aspect of British golf, yet amazingly no allowance whatsoever is currently made for differing climatic conditions when allocating handicaps. This seems illogical, to say the least.

There are essentially three types of golf course in the British Isles. First and foremost, the various seaside links courses dotted around the coast, from Lelant in the far south-west to Reay on the northern shore of Caithness in Scotland. Secondly there are heathland courses, often with lovely springy turf and an abundance of heather and silver birch trees: many of the premier inland courses such as Walton Heath, Sunningdale, Woodhall Spa or Gleneagles belong to this category. Finally come the ubiquitous parkland courses, often based on much heavier clay soils and lined with trees. Such courses range from long-established clubs such as Little Ashton near Birmingham and Moor Park in Hertfordshire, to the recent Belfry complex near Sutton Coldfield. Downfield in Dundee is another particularly impressive and tough parkland test.

Of course not all courses can be neatly slotted into any of these categories; not all courses by the sea are strictly speaking links, and many inland courses (notably Wentworth) combine features from both heathland and parkland golf. Conversely certain courses still retain a seaside-like links flavour, even though the sea may have receded to some distance away. The Australian Sand Belt outside Melbourne provides a spectacular example of this phenomenon overseas, and is described in more detail in a later chapter.

Socially golf in Britain still differs distinctly within the four home countries, even though such differences are not perhaps as pronounced as they once were.

Ireland and Scotland are somewhat similar, for in both countries golf is a truly democratic game, its adherents covering the whole cross-section of society from road-sweepers and dustmen to landowners, judges and the landed gentry. In both countries a low handicap is something of a status symbol: often you hear people in small Scottish towns referred to as if their golf handicap was a direct extension of their character – 'There goes Duncan McKay, works at the distillery, plays off three' – as if no more need to be said.

This democratic flavour is partly because in both Scotland and Ireland the game is still very cheap to play. The annual subscription at most private clubs rarely exceeds £200, with nothing further to pay. Annual

ROYAL ST GEORGES, SANDWICH, ENGLAND▷
A view of the 6th hole with its typical duneland.

◁WENTWORTH, ENGLAND
The 8th hole at Wentworth has a demanding second shot over the water. The heather may make a pretty sight, but it is almost impossible to play a golf shot from it.

ROYAL ST GEORGES,
SANDWICH, ENGLAND▷
This 1st tee has a cunning
device for stacking balls; when
the player arrives he simply
pops his ball in and there is
no dispute about who is to
play.

▽GLENEAGLES,
PERTHSHIRE, SCOTLAND
The four-sided rain shelter on
the King's Course – a welcome
refuge far from the clubhouse.

△ROYAL ABERDEEN,
SCOTLAND
Bunkers were originally
naturally created, first by
rabbits burrowing and then by
wind erosion, and sometimes
by sheep using the hollow as
a shelter. In this picture it is
easy to see how the bunker is
started.

BALLYBUNION, IRELAND▷
The 16th hole at Ballybunion
is one of the country's most
spectacular holes. Here, as the
sun goes down, the wind is
still blowing a fair blast.

◁ROYAL BIRKDALE,
SOUTHPORT, ENGLAND
A plaque commemorates the
great shot played by Arnold
Palmer here on the 16th hole,
on his way to winning the
Open Championship.

21

TURNBERRY, SCOTLAND▷
The 9th tee, rising eighty feet above the rocks and crashing waves, is a dramatic sight but daunting for the player, who has to carry the ball almost two hundred yards to the fairway.

ROYAL ST GEORGES,
SANDWICH, ENGLAND▷
It's common practice in Britain just to turn up and tee-off. It seems not to matter whether you own a Mini or a Rolls-Royce – the clubhouse is avoided until after the round is finished.

Tom Morris died of a broken heart on Christmas Day 1875, aged twenty-four: his wife had died a year earlier in childbirth. During his life he won five Open Championships.

IN MEMORY OF
"TOMMY"
SON OF THOMAS MORRIS
WHO DIED 25TH DECEMBER 1875 AGED 24 YEARS

DEEPLY REGRETTED BY NUMEROUS FRIENDS AND ALL GOLFERS
HE THRICE IN SUCCESSION WON THE CHAMPION'S BELT
AND HELD IT WITHOUT RIVALRY AND YET WITHOUT ENVY
HIS MANY AMIABLE QUALITIES
BEING NO LESS ACKNOWLEDGED THAN HIS GOLFING ACHIEVEMENTS

THIS MONUMENT HAS BEEN ERECTED
BY CONTRIBUTIONS FROM SIXTY GOLFING SOCIETIES

▽ST ANDREWS
A little girl pays for her putting at the Himalayas, the putting green at St Andrews.

dues at municipal (public) courses are even cheaper: the ratepayers of St Andrews enjoy the unique privilege of playing on possibly the most sacred sporting turf in the world for precisely £46 per annum. Within a ten-mile radius of both the two major Scottish cities, Edinburgh and Glasgow, there are no fewer than 40 golf courses of one kind or another, some admittedly fairly primitive. In Scotland everyone plays golf, and it is not uncommon to see whole families playing an evening foursome after tea. For those either too old or too young for the real game there are still the joys of putting, and St Andrews, naturally, possesses the finest of all putting greens, the Himalayas, where on fine summer evenings you can see grandmother and toddler coping with the most extraordinary curls and undulations under the watchful gaze of the Royal and Ancient clubhouse. To this day there survives an annual putting match between the ladies of the St Rule Club and the gentlemen of the R & A – one of the oldest inter-club competitions of all.

In England, and to a lesser extent, in Wales, golf was originally a fairly élitest game, and the only way the ordinary working people could play was through the various artisan sections affiliated to private clubs. In return for performing certain (usually greenskeeping) duties, locals were allowed to play at certain times, mostly during the week or late in the evening. At some of the older, traditional clubs (such as Woking in Surrey or Brancaster in Norfolk) these artisan sections survive, but they are generally becoming a thing of the past. The great majority of private clubs in England and Wales are now reasonably open to all-comers, although the demand for membership still vastly outstrips the places available – hence the lengthy waiting-lists that now seem almost universal. A growing number of golfers in England play their golf not as members of private clubs, but as part of nomadic societies, often organized through business or factory contacts. Parties of from ten to over a hundred enthusiasts will visit private clubs for a day's golf during the week, and their green fees help to keep subscriptions down for their hosts.

Few clubs in Britain have practice grounds or, indeed, anything approaching practice 'facilities' at all. This is partly a reflection of old, entrenched attitudes, suspicious of excessive practice as tantamount to cheating, and partly a simple consequence of lack of space. Times are changing, however, and many cities and some clubs operate their own driving ranges, where the assiduous player can drive balls away for hours on end.

This changing approach to practice is indicative of a much wider shift in the public attitude towards golf as a profession. The status of the professional golfer has risen spectacularly from his early origins as a fairly humble, artisan craftsman, and with the huge rewards now available, many aspiring young players are positively encouraged to turn professional once they have achieved success in the amateur game. Before the Second

GLENEAGLES, PERTHSHIRE, SCOTLAND▷
The par four 15th hole affords a fine view of the golf course, with Glen Devon in the background.

TURNBERRY, SCOTLAND▷▷
An aerial view of the 9th hole, Bruce's Castle, with the lighthouse to the left. Golfers have to go out on to the peninsula tee and hit their drives over the Irish Sea.

WENTWORTH, ENGLAND▷
A view of the 13th hole
doglegged par 4. The heather
is typical of heathland golf
courses.

ROYAL BIRKDALE,
SOUTHPORT, ENGLAND▷
The par 3 12th hole is a long
and spectacular one, where the
only place to be is on the
green.

△DALMUIR, CLYDEBANK, SCOTLAND
Even the most modest golf course has got at least one hole that endears it to the golfers who play there: the par 3 190-yard Gully at Dalmuir is one such.

KILLARNEY, IRELAND▷
The 18th hole on Ross Point is one of the prettiest par 3s in the world. The club is called Killarney Golf and Fishing Club because it has the added advantage of its own lake by the course.

◁KILLARNEY
The 1st hole, a dogleg around the water, is as good an opening hole as can be found anywhere.

31

World War it was unheard of for players to represent Britain both as amateurs (in the Walker Cup) and subsequently as professionals (in the Ryder Cup): since the 1950s this has become almost commonplace, and the 1985 European Ryder Cup team contained no fewer than three players (Sandy Lyle, Paul Way and Howard Clark) who had made such a transition.

The roots of the game of golf undoubtedly lie in Britain. The Royal and Ancient Golf Club is still the ruling authority for the game almost everywhere except the USA. The R & A and the USGA (United States Golf Association) meet regularly to ensure that the rules of both bodies remain, to all intents and purposes, identical. The final disappearance of the small (1.62″) British ball in 1989 will signal the end of perhaps the most obvious discrepancy: the large (1.68″) American ball has been mandatory in all major competitions for many years anyway.

Every golfer should make at least one pilgrimage to the classic courses of Britain, although whether a golfing diet solely restricted to the great championship venues such as St Andrews or Carnoustie is a good idea is not quite so clear. A short drive from these historic circuits are literally dozens of challenging smaller courses that any visitor would greatly enjoy playing. My own course at Erskine, pictured on page 46, is one such, as are Alyth outside Dundee and the splendid seaside links at Elie, south of St Andrews.

Around Britain there are several wonderful seaside courses which, primarily for reasons of remoteness, rarely figure on the itineraries of golfing visitors; you should make every effort to play at, for example, Woodbrook near Dublin or Harlech in North Wales. A quick telephone call to the secretary is usually all it takes to sort out a game, and with careful planning you could spend a wonderful fortnight touring round some of the less-heralded courses of these islands.

In the far north of Scotland, Royal Dornoch has no less than Tom Watson's seal of approval. But to miss the pleasures of nearby Tain would be a great mistake. Further south, in the rolling farmlands of Nairnshire, the championship links of Nairn presents a formidable challenge. The European Oil Capital of Aberdeen also abounds in excellent sport. Cruden Bay and the back-to-back neighbours, Murcar and Royal Aberdeen, more than 200 years old, are a scenic delight and a great test of skill. St Andrews, home of golf, is a Mecca for millions, but how many know that just a ten-minute drive away await the ancient delights of Crail, a short but sharp examination in traditional links golf. In the same Kingdom of Fife, Lundin Links lays claim to one of the best short holes anywhere in golf. 'Perfection' – 160 yards long – is played from an elevated tee to a

ST MELLION, CORNWALL, ENGLAND▷
This early morning view over the 14th hole par 3, with the mist hanging in the valley beyond, shows Cornwall at its best.

34

cunningly bunkered green. The vistas of the Firth of Forth are indelibly etched on my mind.

Over on the west coast of Scotland, it would be impossible to overstate the originality and spectacular beauty of the James Braid creation at Machrihanish in Argyll. It was Braid who also left his imprint on Scotscraig, which lies between Dundee and St Andrews. Edinburgh and Glasgow are each served by more than forty courses. Pollok, adjoining the site of the famed Burrell Art Collection, is one of Glasgow's jewels. And Braid Hills provides a tough challenge as well as unrivalled views over Edinburgh.

Royal Birkdale, scene of so much Open drama, needs no further praise from me. But Lancashire men will not heed the argument that Hillside, an Open qualifying venue, is even more difficult. Formby, another course used for Open qualification, rates almost as highly.

Across the Pennines in Yorkshire, gorse-clad Ganton, which has hosted several major amateur championships, is an unforgettable sight in full bloom. Further south in Manchester the magnificently sculpted parkland at Mere is a must. And St Pierre, Chepstow, is the one stop the European PGA makes in Wales. Its lavish facilities are further reason for paying a visit.

And I can pay no higher compliment to the two Berkshire courses, the Red and the Blue, than state that they are reminiscent of Rosemount in Scotland. And, like Rosemount, they are supremely worthy of a visit.

Britain is fortunate to have little gems of golf courses hidden in every corner of the land. These courses may never get into any top fifty list or even be talked about in the golf media; they are often played only by the local members, and visitors are rare. However the joy for the travelling golfer locating such a course and returning home with memories of it, knowing that he or she is one of the few people to have made such a find, is great.

Many of the golf courses, especially the municipal or city-owned facilities, have only a humble clubhouse or changing facilities. Normally players change their shoes at the car, pay the day's green fees and set off. Some small clubs have a box where visitors are expected to deposit the daily fee, trusting in their honesty and hoping no one steals the box.

The weather is, of course, a serious occupational hazard, but for many people the ever-changing winds and promise of rain are actually part of the fun. As they say at St Andrews, 'If there's nae wind and nae rain it's nae gowf.' The first time you set foot on a seaside links can, even so, be a fairly chastening experience. A lot of people playing the Old Course itself for the first time may wonder what all the fuss is about. Even Bobby Jones, after whom the tenth hole is now named, walked off in disgust after his initial encounter with St Andrews. Yet the Old Course

ROYAL TARLAIR, GRAMPIAN, SCOTLAND▷
Britain's coastline is dotted with golf courses, both on the linksland and the cliff tops. Here at Royal Tarlair the 13th hole plays from one cliff to another, with the North Sea in between.

36

ST ANDREWS, SCOTLAND▷
The Swilcan Bridge, said to have been built by the Romans, spans the burn which runs across the course.

ST ANDREWS▷

A young girl plays with her parents on the Himalayas, the putting course. The annual putting match between the ladies of the St Rule Club and the gentlemen of the Royal and Ancient is one of the oldest tournaments played.

△ST ANDREWS
Royal and Ancient clubhouse and the starter's box.

ROYAL COUNTY DOWN, NEWCASTLE, NORTHERN IRELAND▷
'Where the mountains of Mourne run down to the sea . . .' This Royal course nestles beneath the famed mountains beside the Irish Sea.

◁ST ANDREWS
Some children playing on the mosaic outside the St Andrews Golf Club, which was founded in 1847.

subsequently became Jones's favourite place on earth, and in 1958 he was made a Freeman of the Burgh. The 'old grey town' is that sort of place, and in ordinary (i.e. totally unpredictable) weather the Old Course is still, after four centuries, one of the finest tests of golf anywhere in the world. For the great English golf writer Bernard Darwin, St Andrews was simply the best place for a game of golf. And so it still is. The only trouble nowadays is that virtually every golfer from around the globe seems to think so too!

SUNNINGDALE, BERKSHIRE, ENGLAND▷
The well-manicured clubhouse gardens behind the 18th green show a different aspect of England's most naturally beautiful heathland golf course.

ROYAL BIRKDALE, SOUTHPORT, ENGLAND▷▷
The unkempt areas at Royal Birkdale, with only the tee and green cultivated, are precisely what the Honors Course has taken pains to emulate (see page 7).

ROYAL DORNOCH,
SCOTLAND▷
The 5th hole, photographed
here in the early morning,
typifies the stark beauty of the
course.

▽ ERSKINE, SCOTLAND
The 11th hole is a par 3
playing down towards the
river. This beautiful course,
which lies west of Glasgow
on the banks of the River
Clyde, has been my home
course for a long while now.

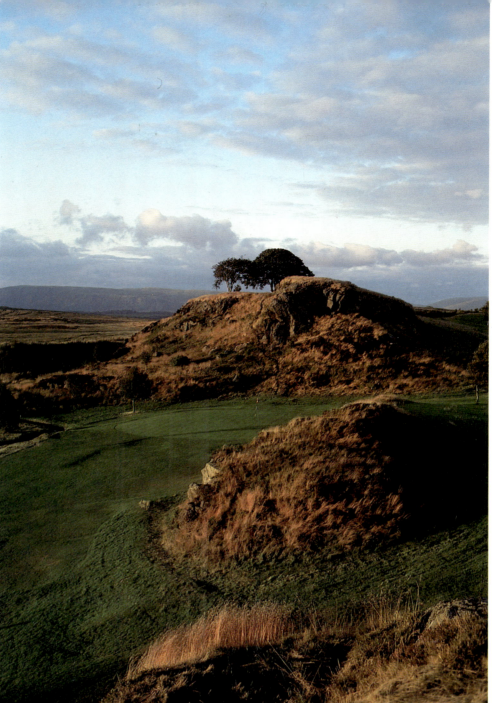

◁WINDYHILL, GLASGOW, SCOTLAND
The par 3 14th hole looks as if it could be a million miles from anywhere; in fact it is only seven miles from the centre of Glasgow.

WATERVILLE, COUNTY KERRY, IRELAND▷
The setting sun gives this view down the 8th hole and over towards the 17th green the air of a lunar landscape.

▽ST ANDREWS, SCOTLAND
The peninsula of linksland jutting out into the estuary of the River Eden contains all four of the St Andrews courses.

European golf is currently enjoying an unprecedented rise in popularity.

To the uneducated it might seem as though we have just discovered the game. In fact, many of the clubs throughout the continent are old and long-established, especially in France and Germany. The Scandinavian countries have the most courses, but facilities for public and private golf are expanding rapidly everywhere.

Brian's photographs show some of the magnificent settings and I hope it will encourage people from around the world to come and sample golf here.

BERNHARD LANGER

CHAMONIX, FRANCE▷

CRANS-SUR-SIERRE, SWITZERLAND▷▷
The Alps in this glorious early morning light make a perfect backdrop for one of the highest golf courses in the world.

EUROPE

Golf is now an accepted pastime in almost every European country, and one sometimes forgets that until recently it was widely regarded as an eccentric amusement of the very rich. (In France at one time golf was considered so accurate an indication of extreme wealth that tax returns specifically asked whether or not you played golf!) Things are changing very rapidly, but only perhaps in Sweden is the game yet reaching the masses. Throughout Europe golf course construction is proceeding apace, partly of course inspired by the exploits of players like Severiano Ballesteros and Bernhard Langer, who have provided highly successful models for their fellow-countrymen to emulate.

In architectural terms, the courses of northern Europe are naturally heavily influenced by British examples, and distinct 'national' variations are rather difficult to discern. The coastline of Europe has several splendid seaside links of the traditional type, Falsterbo in Sweden and Kennemer in Holland being two of the most distinguished. Indeed at Kennemer you could be forgiven for thinking that you were among the sandhills of Sandwich or Birkdale, whilst Falsterbo offers a classic test in the flat, windswept Scottish manner. The latter offers a graphic example of the relatively democratic nature of golf in Sweden, as reference to the photograph on page 69 will show. Compare the bicycle park for the members at Falsterbo with the opulence of the car park at Falkenstein, West Germany – almost an outdoor showroom for Mercedes. In many ways golf in Sweden provides the closest approximation to the British pattern to be found on the Continent, and the game is currently growing at an extraordinary rate. The emergence of Swedish professionals such as Mats Lanner can only foreshadow a time when the European Ryder Cup team is studded with Scandinavian players.

The biggest problems confronting golf in Sweden are inevitably geographical; the long winter nights, extremes of cold, and persistent damp do not provide an ideal environment for the proper upkeep of courses, and Sweden is almost certainly unique in the widespread adoption of a studded wellington boot as standard golfing footwear. Nevertheless there are times when even the hardiest golf addict is forced to retreat indoors, and the resourceful Scandinavians have adapted a version of the game to their restricting surroundings: computer graphics are used to plot the flight of balls hit towards a photographic screen, and each year the World Indoor Golf Championship is held amidst intense competition.

For many Britons, however, the vision of golf on the Contintent is rather more tropical and idyllic; an oasis of lush, watered fairways, brilliant white sand and rolling greens in which to escape from the rigours of the

CHAMONIX, FRANCE▷
The relatively flat 18th hole is in stark contrast to the Alpine scenery.

VIMIERO, PORTUGAL▷
Driving off the elevated tee, with a river to the right and a road to the left, makes for a difficult start.

CHANTILLY, FRANCE▷
Hole number 13, the par 4 that plays over a gully to the green.

△PENINA, PORTUGAL
The 18th hole pictured as the sun goes down. Henry Cotton designed this course and lived here for several years.

REYKJAVIK, ICELAND▷
A general view over the course from the hills above the town. From a distance the tundra looks colourless and bland, but it is in fact extremely colourful with flowers of many varieties growing there.

◁FALKENSTEIN, HAMBURG, GERMANY
The deep bunkering on the 2nd hole is typical of this inland course.

golfing winter at home. This of course means the Iberian Peninsula – Spain and, increasingly, Portugal.

Southern Spain is the major holiday destination for winter golfers throughout northern Europe, and endless charter flights ship players to a few celebrated – and ever more crowded – locations. Throughout Spain and Portugal golf complexes with timeshare and retirement houses attached are emerging, to cater for the growing number of golfers wishing to enjoy the mild winter climate on a rather more permanent basis. It seems very likely that the enormous boom in such properties experienced in Florida and southern California will soon be repeated in southern Europe.

Opportunities for the indigenous population of Spain and Portugal to play golf nonetheless remain slim, as increasing demand pushes green fees ever higher, quite beyond the reach of ordinary local people: block-booking of starting times by package tour operators during the popular winter season means that in any case access to a course is extremely restricted. Despite the existence of a few brilliant stars, including not just the greatest player in the world today, Severiano Ballesteros, but also the highly promising former Amateur Champion, José-Maria Olazabal, it is not perhaps to Spain that one should look for a genuine cohort of young native talent. Many experienced observers consider Sweden or West Germany altogether more fertile ground for development. We shall see.

Meanwhile, from Normandy to Nice, France is the envy of her golfing neighbours. Few other countries in Europe have so many old established clubs on such a varying landscape. The northern coast of France is only 21 miles from England and golf was brought across the Channel by British visitors at about the turn of the century. France is a beautiful country for golf and, although it only has a modest number of courses per capita, most regions of the country have places to play. The differing landscapes, from the gently rolling hills around Paris to the alpine backdrop of Chamonix and south to the shores of the Mediterranean, give France a special quality.

Paris in the spring has always had an appeal, but add a few rounds of golf on the magnificent courses around the city to be sure of an unforgettable stay. Everyone associates wine with France, but few people have enjoyed golfing in the southern valleys, where after the day's activities on the course players can enjoy a visit to the vineyards and sample the local produce. Whether you stay a week or a month you will run out of different courses to play long before you run out of vintages to sample. While the current explosion of golf in Europe means that a large number of courses are under construction in France, the majority of the courses there are well established. Like Britain, the clubs are mostly solely for golf with few facilities for anything else. The clubhouses are generally

FALKENSTEIN, HAMBURG, GERMANY▷
The par 4 13th hole plays up the hill to an elevated green, reminiscent of Sunningdale in England.

60

△CRANS-SUR-SIERRE,
SWITZERLAND

△CHANTILLY, FRANCE
Golf clubhouses around the
world range from shacks to
elegant châteaux. Pictured
here are some of the varied
styles to be found in Europe.
Examples from around
America may be seen on
pages 190 and 191.

KENNEMER, HOLLAND▷

△KONINKLIJKE, BELGIUM

VALE DE LOBO, PORTUGAL▷
The spectacular cliff-top 16th
hole; the evening sun turns the
rocky cliff face to gold.

◁FALKENSTEIN, HAMBURG,
GERMANY

impressive old buildings with superb dining rooms and lounges.

Switzerland has only a few courses and the playing season is relatively short. The mountainous terrain makes building a good course difficult but, where courses do exist, they are sure to be spectacular. Crans-sur-Sierre is Switzerland's best-known course, primarily because it has for many years hosted the Swiss Open. Crans, a small skiing town halfway up a mountain, signifies the best of golf in this country. It is similar to Vail in Colorado, with expensive shops and elegant restaurants. The golf course is modest in length for this altitude but the views from every hole on the course, looking around and up to the mountains, are unrivalled.

The demand for golf in Europe is growing so fast that many courses have had to introduce special restrictions so that playing is not delayed by beginners to the game. It is not uncommon for players to have to be passed by a professional before being allowed out on the course. The pro would normally teach the individual for several weeks and introduce him or her to the etiquette of the game before allowing them out on the hallowed turf. The Germans take a typically regimental approach to the game and practise as instructed by their teacher. One lady who turned up as if for a dental appointment at precisely 3 p.m. every Tuesday was just not picking up the game at all. She knew all the rules and was second to none as far as etiquette was concerned, but she could only rarely make connection with the ball. One day the pro decided to take her out on the course but, when they reached a short par 4 with a pond in front of the green, the lady's ball kept landing in the water. After three failed attempts to carry the pond the pro reached into her golf bag for yet another ball, but instead pulled out a plastic bag containing a clump of grass. 'What's this?' inquired the pro. 'Ah, that is my provisional divot,' answered the woman, 'I'm always afraid I'll lose mine, so I carry a spare!' This story in some ways illustrates the enthusiasm and intensity of the game in Europe. No matter how many obstacles or how inconvenient the game becomes, the golfer will overcome the trials and tribulations set before him to be allowed to play.

Italy, famous for the canals of Venice and the grandeur of Rome, does not conjure up thoughts of rolling fairways, but the country not only has many fine courses, but they are located in the most unlikely places. Who would have thought that both of these fine cities would have the facilities for the Royal and Ancient game within a short distance of the centres? Like France, Italy has courses from the Alps to the blistering Mediterranean shore. With its group of courses in the southern provinces where the winter climate allows warm winter play, it must surely only be a matter of time before, like the south coast of Spain, golfing European sun-seekers discover another area for development.

If Italy seems an unlikely location for golf, then what is to be said

BIELLA, ITALY▷
The 16th hole plays out of the narrow shoot on to the elevated fairway. The drive has to be played just short of this steep sloping hill, and the second shot is as it can be seen in the picture.

PALS, COSTA BRAVA, SPAIN▷
The crowded practice ground shows that there is plenty of enthusiasm for the game in this part of the world.

△IGLS, INNSBRUCK, AUSTRIA
Golfers starved of courses in Austria have to make do with any piece of spare ground on which to hit balls. Here a small field outside a hotel has been turned into a summertime practice facility.

▽FALKENSTEIN, HAMBURG, GERMANY
It couldn't be anywhere else in the world – a car park full of Mercedes.

△FLOMMEN, SWEDEN
In this part of the world, where
the golf courses are seldom
dry, players wear boots with
golf studs in them. These golf
boots are made in Sweden but
can be bought elsewhere in
Europe.

▽FALSTERBO, SWEDEN
A contrast to the Mercedes in
Germany: bicycles lined up
while their owners enjoy an
afternoon round of golf.

△AKUREYRI, ICELAND
On my visit to Akureyri I was
fortunate to have this former
Miss Iceland as my caddie –
her husband was playing in the
group ahead.

of Iceland? The land of the midnight sun is not, as its name suggests, a land of ice, but instead is only a few hundred miles north of Scotland. While the landscape is barren, with few trees, the tundra on close inspection contains hundreds of tiny coloured flowers of varying shapes and sizes. Long dark winters prohibit the enjoyment of the game for many months; however, this is more than made up for by the long summer evenings – then play is possible twenty-four hours a day. Here and Alaska are the only places boasting a midnight golf tournament. The courses have to contend with a rough landscape and tough winters, but they survive quite well. And the visiting golfer will find hospitality unequalled, no matter how far he travels. The local Icelanders are proud of their country and will drink you under the table given half a chance.

The current explosion of golf in and around Europe has had a dramatic effect on the professional golf tour there. No longer have players to travel to the lucrative tournaments in the USA to make themselves famous or even just highly paid individuals. The United States professional golf tour still offers the highest rewards, but with the falling value of the dollar and the rise in European purses, several tournaments are now on a par in cash value with their American counterparts. The day cannot be far away when one of the European events will actually be worth more than the concurrent event across the Atlantic.

Ryder Cup matches in recent years have given world golf a perspective on Europe as a breeding ground for players of outstanding ability. Names such as Woosnam, Brown, Torrance and Olazabal have been added to the better-known major tournament winners, Faldo, Langer, Lyle and Ballesteros, and American players no longer expect to win when pitted against even the least-known players.

I firmly believe players finishing their college golf education in America would do well to follow the example of established stars like Payne Stewart and give the European circuit a try before committing all their efforts to the tour at home. Playing golf throughout Europe, these players would find courses not quite up to the general standard enjoyed in America and, battling with wind and rain, would have to learn shots not usually required back home. The constant change in cultures and the difficulties of dealing with people of differing nationalities, coupled with the hectic cross-country travel, all combine to build character essential in the successful tournament player.

Some of the more learned players on the US tour make regular forays into Europe, for it is often the case that a complete change can rejuvenate their game. It is also more likely that they will find themselves in contention where the depth of quality players is not yet at the level encountered at home. With Australia and the Far East also enjoying

PALS, COSTA BRAVA, SPAIN▷
The par 3 11th hole, from an elevated tee and through a very narrow gap in the trees, although quite short is nevertheless one of the most challenging holes on the course.

MONTE CARLO, MONACO▷▷
The golf course sits on the mountain top behind Monte Carlo, but the only hole with a view of the town below is the par 3 14th.

huge increases in the numbers playing golf, the day of the World Golf Tour cannot be far away. When that happens, Europe will surely have more than its fair share of events.

Travelling around Europe recently, I was pleasantly surprised to discover the impact golf is now having on even the least sports-conscious sectors of society. In every fashionable High Street boutique there are examples of golf knitwear, shirts and accessories, usually emblazoned with an appropriate logo, be it 'Golf Country Club' (as in France), or simply a variation of the crossed-clubs motto used on golf club shields everywhere. It is no coincidence that Volkswagen christened their up-market hatchback 'Golf', as throughout Europe the word seems to denote a certain class and style, rather similar to the connotations of 'Polo' in the United States.

The quality and condition of the best European courses cannot be improved upon anywhere in the world. Many of the clubs are run by, and for, the most influential local businessmen and notables (even beyond the Iron Curtain), and therefore have superb facilities. There is considerable social kudos attached to membership of a golf club, even where, rarely, enthusiasm for the game itself is limited. The demand for experienced professional advice is phenomenal, and once the outdoor season is completed many professionals simply switch to coaching indoors.

Although the game is undoubtedly taking off throughout Europe, there are still many obstacles to be overcome before golf can begin to match the popularity of, say, tennis. One major problem is the strong opposition among conservationists to the use of precious land for possibly 'decadent' ends; few seem to understand that a properly designed and cared-for golf course provides one of the best environments for natural wildlife and flora. This antagonism has created the absurd situation, by no means unique to West Germany, in which clubs exist, each with a thriving membership and appropriate property, but are unable for want of planning permission to construct an actual course.

This account of golf in Europe must, however, end on an optimistic note. With the recent triumphs of European golfers, particularly in the United States, the game is getting even more publicity and is sure to continue booming here for many years to come.

IGLS, INNSBRUCK, AUSTRIA▷
The 18th hole, with the little village of Rinn and the snow-capped Alps peeking out above the low-lying cloud.

△VIMIERO, PORTUGAL
The bridge from the 1st green to the 2nd tee spans the river which runs through the course.

△KONINKLIJKE, BELGIUM
One of the few motorized golf carts in Belgium even bears local licence plates.

VIMIERO▷
Women working on their hands and knees to remove even the smallest blemish from the greens.

△FALSTERBO, SWEDEN
A young boy shows off some of his cache of golf balls retrieved from one of the lakes on the course.

FALSTERBO▷
The 18th hole runs right alongside the dunes but has some protection from the wind – unlike most of the rest of the course, which is extremely exposed.

◁PALS, COSTA BRAVA, SPAIN
The chief caddie instructs younger members of staff in the technique. Some of these youngsters may follow in the footsteps of Seve Ballesteros, who started in a similar fashion.

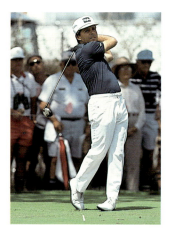

What more can one say about golf in a country like South Africa that enjoys such scenic natural beauty and an average 220 days of sunshine a year? Anyone who has played or followed South Africa's Sunshine Circuit held during the magnificent summer months of November to January will bear witness to this. It alone probably explains the unusually high number of players and courses in a country with a relatively small population. Among these courses are some that still rank among my personal favourites in the world. Brian's elegant photography is sufficient testimony to any accusation that in my case I am letting sentiment override objectivity!

But the outdoor lifestyle isn't the only reason that accounts for the healthy state of golf in South Africa. Beyond the actual golf-playing community, support and interest in the game by the public-at-large are high. So much so, that South Africa can boast as one of its achievements the first ever million-dollar tournament in the world. Great variations in altitude give rise to an interesting variety of conditions and the cost of playing is extremely low due to the subsidization by corporations of private clubs. Also, the courses tend to be concentrated in specific areas which makes travel between them extremely easy.

Golf wasn't made in South Africa. But it certainly could have been made *for* South Africa.

I've also been fortunate enough to play golf in India and other parts of the great continent of Africa. The courses, mostly founded by British expatriates, are varied and wonderful and continue the traditions of the game, with Royal Calcutta being the oldest club outside the British Isles.

GARY PLAYER

ROYAL CAPE, CAPE TOWN, SOUTH AFRICA▷

AFRICA, INDIA AND THE ARAB STATES

△MILNERTON GOLF CLUB,
CAPE TOWN, SOUTH AFRICA
The caddie compound where
every day the caddies gather
to serve the golfers.

MILNERTON GOLF CLUB▷
The city of Cape Town with
Table Mountain behind is
almost lost in the haze as the
wind blows the surf back
behind the 5th green.

The huge continent that is Africa almost certainly has the lowest density of golf courses and golfers of any substantial landmass in the world – only the Soviet Union is a true golfing desert. Even so there are few African countries which have not, at one time or another, enjoyed golf in some form, and needless to say those courses that do exist provide golf of infinite variety.

The massive contrasts within the African landscape dictate a fairly flexible attitude to course architecture, as can be seen from the photographs. As in South America, golf was originally a British import, brought in by the soldiers, administrators, engineers and businessmen who staffed the old Empire. Golfers, like Victorian mission-aries, took their beloved sport to every corner of the land and, despite the gradual dissolution of the British Empire, many clubs still betray strong traces of a colonial past. African golf remains very much the domain of the rich and privileged, and in certain areas settler tea-planters, ranch owners and financiers have managed to create clubs and courses of a standard equivalent to anything in Britain. Where the political structure has been overturned, as in Zimbabwe (formerly Rhodesia), the game survives almost unchanged. The establishment of majority rule has opened up a few distinguished clubs (like the Royal Harare, formerly Royal Salisbury Golf Club) to black members, but these are themselves part of the new black ruling élite, and hardly representative of the populace at large.

Thirteen times Open Champion of his own country, and winner of no fewer than nine of golf's major titles, Gary Player has been perhaps the most potent sporting ambassador for South African golf. He has always worked for a completely integrated sporting system, and has played golf the world over, encouraging people at least to take a look at the South African situation for themselves, before jumping to any conclusions. As Gary says in his introduction to this book, the world's first million-dollar golf tournament actually took place in one of the black homeland states of South Africa, and his example, and that of players like Vincent Tshabalala, should help to break down those sporting barriers that still exist among the peoples of South Africa.

Moving further north and east towards the oilfields of the Persian Gulf, the virtual absence of grassland has meant that avid golfers have had to adapt to the unsuitable terrain in the most unlikely ways. Courses in, for example, Saudi Arabia or the United Arab Emirates are built almost entirely on sand, mixed with oil and baked by the sun to provide natural contours for bunkers and 'greens'. These putting surfaces are rolled and prepared very carefully, and then covered with a thin film of

ROYAL NEPAL, KATMANDHU, NEPAL▷
One of the roughest pieces of ground ever to boast a golf course still manages to excite the eye. Note the Buddhist monastery half-hidden in the distance.

84

△DUBAI, UNITED ARAB
EMIRATES
Astroturf tees are ingeniously
constructed to give elevation
and character on this all-sand
golf course.

△DUBAI
A player uses his square of
astroturf. The rules allow the
ball to be placed immediately
behind on the artificial surface,
provided that it lands on
fairway marked by boundary
posts.

◁ROYAL NEPAL,
KATMANDHU, NEPAL
The greenskeeper waters his
only grass green; all the other
'greens' are made of a mixture
of sand and oil.

GOKARNA SAFARI PARK,
KATMANDHU, NEPAL▷
Caddies prepare the green for
a player to putt.

ROYAL CALCUTTA, INDIA▷
Women from the highly
populated area surrounding
the courses, where running
water is at a premium, find a
use for the deep water hazards
on the golf course, seemingly
unaware of the well-dressed
golfers playing above.

sand, which is smoothed over by each group after holing out. Every player carries a small square of astroturf and, having driven, places this under the ball for his second and subsequent shots from the 'fairway'. A series of posts demarcate this area, and if you stray beyond this zone you have to play the ball where it lies, without using your piece of astroturf.

The putting surfaces on these desert courses are excellent, and the greenskeeping staff take great pride in their 'browns', as they are commonly called. Desert golf may seem, to anyone brought up on lush, manicured fairways, a higher form of lunacy. To its aficionados it is, nevertheless, absolutely true to the original, simple spirit of the game.

Whilst the natural problems of growing the first grass course in Dubai, at the Emirates Golf Club, are if anything extreme, these pioneers certainly don't lack confidence, and they are even creating, alongside the fairways, the hand-built caddy-cart paths familiar at many American country clubs. A million-dollar clubhouse, styled like the tents of Arabian nomads, is being constructed, and where else in the world will you be able to play eighteen holes in the morning, watch camel racing in the afternoon, and round off with a quick dip in the Persian Gulf at your favourite beach club in the evening? Life for the oil tycoon, despite temperatures in excess of 120°F, is not too bad!

Golf on the Indian sub-continent has much in common with the game in Africa. It too was originally a British innovation, and the golf clubs of the Raj were often the last word in opulence and luxury for the favoured few. The political upheavals of the last forty years have not, however, been nearly such a threat to the development of golf as the simple pressure of feeding and housing one of the densest concentrations of population in the world. Many clubs and courses have retreated behind very circumscribed boundaries, and this has if anything reinforced the sense that golf is an upper-class preserve, rather than a game for the people as a whole. To those outside the club confines, the daily challenge of scraping enough to eat to avoid starvation must take precedence over the task of hitting a minute white ball into a small hole in the ground.

Whilst the Raj has gone, the surviving clubs still function as social centres for the local notables, and many continue to thrive. The abundance of cheap labour in India means that such institutions still employ an army of servants, who perform every conceivable menial task for their masters and mistresses. Things have changed since Independence in 1947, but not perhaps so much if some of these former bastions of the Empire are anything to go by. Quite how Indian golf will develop over the next few decades is open to question, and here, possibly more than anywhere else, there is a strong sense that the game is at the mercy of external pressures which may, or may not, prove damaging to its future health. Golf in India can be a wonderful experience for those lucky enough to get a game, but as to whether this will last, only time can tell.

DUBAI, UNITED ARAB EMIRATES▷
The wind paints a wavelike pattern on the sand which constitutes the fairway of a par 3 hole on this golf course in the sand.

△ROYAL NEPAL,
KATMANDHU, NEPAL
The clubhouse.

GOKARNA SAFARI PARK,
KATMANDHU▷
Golf courses around the globe
are host to all sorts of animals,
but there are not many where
you are liable to encounter an
elephant as big as this.

Golf in Australia and New Zealand comes as close to the traditional British game as anything in the world. The climate provides the one, important, difference, and in parts of Australasia golf is essentially a winter game. Summer temperatures may exceed 100°F, and the absence of electric carts can make eighteen holes a real test of endurance. In consequence many golf trolleys, or trundlers as the Australians call them, are equipped with a small seat upon which to rest between shots.

As in Britain, the premier clubs in Australia and New Zealand are essentially *golf* clubs, with few added frills. There are none of the swimming pools, tennis courts or other luxuries deemed necessary in the USA. Professional shops are usually small, but well equipped, and the club professional will carry out everything from minor club repairs to instruction and basic maintenance.

Despite the heat, Australian golf is generally played at a brisk pace, largely because it has always remained a match-play game, with stroke play confined to regular medal days. Needless to say the Australian golfer will have developed a considerable thirst during the round, and it is not unknown for a few 'tinnies' to be added to the contents of his trolley, along with a small bucket of soil and sand used for replacing divots.

Both Australia and New Zealand are blessed with many fine courses, some of a very great age, and the composite layout at Royal Melbourne is high on most people's list of their top ten courses in the world. Royal Melbourne was originally designed by Alister Mackenzie, the architect behind Augusta, and utilizes the wonderful natural opportunities provided by the unique geological phenomenon of the 'Sand Belt', a virtually continuous chain of golf courses around the outskirts of Melbourne. The stately grandeur of the premier Australian clubs contrasts markedly with the more spartan version of golf played in the outback and the hills of New Zealand, but enthusiasm for the game is the same everywhere.

Many great players of the past have emerged from Australia, notably Peter Thomson, five times Open Champion, and Kel Nagle, who won the Centenary Open at St Andrews in 1960. When Greg Norman triumphed at Turnberry in 1986, he became the fourth Antipodean golfer to join this illustrious roll of honour, the great New Zealander Bob Charles having secured the only left-handed victory in the entire history of the Open Championship, at Lytham in 1963.

As one travels north from Australia and New Zealand, the golf becomes as exotic as the names of the islands might suggest. Fiji, Samoa, Tahiti

AWANA GOLF CLUB, GENTING HIGHLANDS, MALAYSIA▷
The tropical foliage and densely covered hills add to the beauty of this golf course situated halfway up a mountain.

PARAPURUMA BEACH, WELLINGTON, NEW ZEALAND▷▷
The par 5 6th hole, which plays uphill with a backdrop of mountains, belies the course name, for although it is a links course close to the beach, it affords no view of the sea.

DISCOVERY BAY, HONG
KONG▷
The 9th hole on this
mountainous course. The
resort, three miles from Hong
Kong Island, is served by
hydrofoil.

▽SINGAPORE ISLAND GOLF
CLUB, SINGAPORE
With almost ten thousand
members, the club is the
largest in the Far East and its
four courses are always busy.

△TITIRANGI, AUCKLAND, NEW ZEALAND
The 14th hole on this magnificent course, designed by Alister Mackenzie.

PACIFIC HARBOUR, FIJI▷
The 15th par 5 dogleg – a hole cut out of the jungle where the errant shot disappears for ever – is one of the most dramatic holes on this famous course.

◁AWANA GOLF CLUB, GENTING HIGHLANDS, MALAYSIA
A topiary tiger overlooks the 1st green, practice ground and clubhouse.

101

and Bali conjure up all sorts of delightful visions, and even the most jaded golfer might be stirred by the thought of a game at, say, the Royal Samoa Golf Club.

In Britain almost all the 'Royal' clubs have championship courses of great antiquity and distinction. In the South Seas, however, the 'Royal' prefix may simply indicate that a club is the local, indeed the only, course of an island potentate. Royal Samoa, for example, has only twelve fairly primitive holes, but the setting is absolutely delightful. Royal patronage of the golf club is marked by a special space for the King, highlighted by small white stones, in the grass car park.

Tahiti has only one modest layout, but Fiji is rather better endowed. The main course in the capital itself is flat and not very interesting, but a couple of hours away lies the beautiful and testing Pacific Harbour golf course, by any standards a wonderful place for a game.

Even the delights of Pacific Harbour are dwarfed, however, by the experience of golf in Bali, which possesses one of the most remarkable courses I have ever seen. Having flown into Denpasa I was driven for two hours through the mud and rain of the Balinese jungle to the 'resort' of Bali Handara. Since I arrived in total darkness the whole place seemed somewhat mysterious, almost threatening, but when I awoke the next morning I was greeted by one of the finest golfing views in the whole world. From the veranda of my bedroom I gazed out at what can only be described as the Garden of Eden, except that this paradise was dotted with tees and greens! Clouds hung from the surrounding mountains like icing on a cake, and the small lake to my right glistened in the morning sun: banks of flowers added to the beauty of the scene, and I could hardly wait to get cracking with my camera! The course itself was in quite superb condition, with probably the best fairway bunkering I have ever seen, and its relative remoteness means that it is unlikely ever to become over-played. A game at Bali Handara is an absolute must for the golfing visitor to the South Seas.

Further northwards both Malaysia and Singapore offer some excellent golf. The country club on Singapore Island has no fewer than ten thousand members, and across the bay lies Sentosa Golf Club, enjoying a magnificent view of down-town Singapore. There are strong Japanese business interests in both Malaysia and Singapore, and numerous Japanese golfers belong to clubs in the islands. Malaysia, and in particular the capital Kuala Lumpur, is well equipped for golf, and the Royal Selangor Golf Club is perhaps the finest test, with its unique short 17th, a drive over water to a green modelled on the famous Redan at North Berwick in Scotland. Away from the capital and up in the mountains lies the extraordinary Awana Golf Club, part of the casino resort of Genting Highlands, 4000 feet above sea level. Awana has been literally hacked from the jungle and, once the early morning mist has cleared, reveals

△ROYAL SYDNEY,
AUSTRALIA
The British-style clubhouses
of the Royal Sydney and the
Royal Hong Kong are in
marked contrast to the modern
design of the new clubhouse
at Tamsui Golf Club, Taiwan.

◁ROYAL HONG KONG,
HONG KONG

TAHITI▷
The 18th hole looks lush and
inviting in the late afternoon
sun at Tahiti, where no golfer
could fail to enjoy this tropical
paradise.

▽TAIWAN GOLF AND
COUNTRY CLUB, TAIWAN

NEW SOUTH WALES,
AUSTRALIA▷
The Australian coastline also
has many golf courses with
views over the ocean. Alister
Mackenzie designed this
course, close to the point
where Captain Cook made his
landing.

▽ANGELSEY GOLF CLUB,
ANGELSEY, AUSTRALIA
Kangaroos look on like
interested spectators as golfers
play all around them.

◁BARWON HEADS,
MELBOURNE, AUSTRALIA
The old pro Bud Russell looks
out over his links. The former
Englishman has been the
professional here for over
twenty-five years.

▽ROTORUA, NEW ZEALAND
The bubbling sulphur pool
doesn't appear to deter the
golfers on this 9-hole course.

△NEW SOUTH WALES,
SYDNEY, AUSTRALIA
Golfers carry small buckets of
sand and seed with them to
repair the damage.

△BALI HANDARA, INDONESIA
The unusual Aztec-like entrance to the club.

BALI HANDARA▷
The mountainous backdrop to the 16th hole gives a glimpse of the fact that this area was formerly a volcano. The resulting rich soil makes the course a positive Garden of Eden.

itself to be another little golfing gem, with some of the tightest driving holes anywhere. A cautious iron from the tee, rather than a full-blooded swipe with a driver, is probably the best policy at Awana. Needless to say the views from both course and clubhouse are quite out of this world.

Heading ever nearer to mainland China, we must first stop in Taiwan, where at Old Tamsui the Taiwan Country Club possesses a lovely course overlooking the estuary. In many Asian clubs female caddies are the norm, but not at Old Tamsui, and several fine male players have risen through the caddie ranks, notably the Chen brothers and, from a slightly older generation, the famous 'Mr Lu', Lian Huan Lu, who so nearly won the Open at Birkdale in 1971. There are more than fourteen courses dotted around Taiwan, and the game, although essentially the preserve of the rich and privileged, is becoming increasingly popular. Mind you, there are still notices around 'kindly asking members to ensure that their chauffeurs do not enter the clubhouse', so perhaps the advance of golfing democracy in Taiwan still has a little way to go!

Hong Kong is our next port of call, and obviously any remarks about golf in the Crown Colony must be somewhat provisional, with the shift to Chinese control due in 1997. All the signs are, however, that really important things like golf will stay much as they are. As one might expect, the game in Hong Kong is very British in character, and the three courses of the enormous Royal Hong Kong Golf Club would not be at all out of place back home.

The chronic shortage of land in the province has forced golf enthusiasts and developers to be more and more inventive architecturally, and two courses have opened recently high up on the hills above Hong Kong Harbour. Clearwater Bay, forty-five minutes by car from the city centre, or alternatively a short helicopter ride, is literally a hilly peninsula with the top sliced off and flattened to accommodate the fairways. Go slightly off line at Clearwater Bay and your ball will drop gracefully into the Pacific, several hundred feet below. Discovery Bay also sits up in the clouds, and is reached by hydrofoil and car in about thirty minutes from Hong Kong harbour. At both Discovery Bay and Clearwater electric carts have been imported, to help golfers struggling with the hilly terrain.

Needless to say the demand for membership of golf clubs in Hong Kong is colossal, and the cost of corporate membership at the Royal Hong Kong Golf Club comes to well over $1 million. It will be fascinating to see whether the Chinese take-over alters the situation in any way, and certainly the official encouragement now given to the game by the People's Republic suggests that some at least of that vast landmass will be given over to golf. Nearly a dozen courses now exist on mainland China, but the first, and probably still the finest, is the wonderful layout at the resort of Chung Shan Hot Springs, just over one hour's ride by hovercraft from Hong Kong.

CHUNG SHAN HOT SPRINGS, CHINA▷
At the uphill par 4 7th hole, looking back towards the clubhouse. The course was carved out of this rolling terrain by means of only the most primitive mechanical aids.

SENTOSA, SINGAPORE▷▷
The spectacular 14th hole at Sentosa runs right to the water's edge and almost into down-town Singapore.

△FIJI GOLF CLUB, FIJI
One of the barefooted caddies
attends the flag.

NEW TAMSUI GOLF CLUB,
TAIWAN▷
The caddie passes a burial
ground, many of which are to
be found beside the courses
in this part of the world.

116

△TAHITI
The English professional at Tahiti, here teaching a group of school children all about the game.

△SAMOA
Who could resist buying balls from this semi-naked child at the edge of the Golf Club in Samoa?

117

Chung Shan Hot Springs was designed by Arnold Palmer on fabulous terrain, and virtually all the construction work was done by hand, an enormous operation involving thousands of labourers, many of whom still tend to the daily upkeep of the course. A river runs through the centre, and numerous retaining walls, roads, paths and bridges had to be constructed, in addition to the magnificent clubhouse. Flowers have been planted all round the course, and even shaped into the club logo. Actual greenskeeping equipment may be a little primitive, but the abundance of labour enables the authorities always to keep Chung Shan in superb condition. The professional, Peter Tang, originates from Hong Kong and is gradually building up a team of highly talented Chinese youngsters. Peter is a very fine player, but both he and I were quite put to shame by one of his girl pupils, who joined our match and began with five birdies in the first nine holes.

Among Peter Tang's older pupils are several top politicians from Beijing (Peking), and with any luck they will catch the golfing bug and spread the word among their colleagues. One wonders how long it will be before China produces a golfer to challenge the world. At present the game is still to some extent viewed as an exotic foreign implant, primarily for resident Japanese and American executives, and this impression is reinforced by the importation of electric carts and other luxuries. Nevertheless the desire for change in the People's Republic is such that no one can confidently predict what the future might bring, and the day will come when thousands of grey-smocked Chinese may be seen hitting balls into the night sky over Beijing. It's a nice thought, anyway.

One could spend years travelling through Australasia and the Far East in search of ever-more unlikely and exotic golf courses. I'm sure that as a result of this book I will receive outraged letters from several clubs in some of the remote hills and mountains, wondering why they have been left out. Once again, I have tried to include a representative selection, and to highlight some of the particular golfing specialities of the region.

With temperatures regularly in excess of 100°F, and over 90 per cent humidity, golf in the South Pacific is not a game for the faint-hearted. Palatial clubhouses and electric carts are very much the exception, and much of the golf here is elemental in the extreme. To many people that is of course a great part of its charm, and certainly the absence of facilities that we Westerners take for granted does not seem to have impeded many highly promising youngsters from making their names in the golfing world at large. Few experts would, I think, be surprised if the first Asian winner of a major championship emerged not from Japan but from Malaysia, Taiwan or the Philippines.

CARAMUNDEL, NEW ZEALAND▷
With electrified fences preventing their ruining the greens, sheep are allowed the freedom of the course and assist in maintenance by keeping the fairway grass cropped.

NEW TAMSUI GOLF CLUB,
TAIWAN▷

A study in headgear. At New Tamsui, the girl caddies wear traditional coolie hats, while the greenskeeper at Malaysia is well protected from the sun. The woman caddie cleaning golf balls at the Royal Hong Kong is wearing a traditional Hakka hat.

▽ROYAL HONG KONG,
HONG KONG

△AWANA GOLF CLUB,
GENTING HIGHLANDS,
MALAYSIA

◁TAHITI
The greens superintendent, out for his afternoon round of golf.

AWANA GOLF CLUB, GENTING HIGHLANDS, MALAYSIA▷
The 2nd hole, a downhill par 4, runs along a narrow finger of land, with steep slopes on either side falling away to the dense jungle.

◁▽SAMOA
The caddies start young in these parts: a cheerful group wait for business at Samoa, and the one below at Fiji is not much bigger than the cart itself.

▽FIJI GOLF CLUB, FIJI

121

However, there are still thousands of square miles in the East almost completely devoid of golf, and huge opportunities for development exist. The Japanese influence is strong, and it can only be a matter of time before the Japanese golf boom spreads south among the islands of the Pacific. Without doubt Australasia and the Far East contain some of the finest courses in the world, and I hope that the pictures convey some of the delights of my own favourites, like Chung Shan Hot Springs or Bali Handara. The only real problem confronting golf in this part of the world at the moment is that, if you will excuse the pun, there are just not enough courses to go round!

CLEARWATER BAY, HONG KONG▷
The 5th hole doesn't leave much room for error – thousands of balls are lost in the sea each year.

NEW TAMSUI GOLF CLUB,
TAIWAN▷
The only way to get to the
18th tee is in a mini railway-
car, and it certainly saves a
very hard climb.

▽CLEARWATER BAY,
HONG KONG
The clubhouse, with the partly
constructed 2nd nine being
fashioned from the hilltop
above.

△HONG KONG,
A player heads for Discovery
Bay by hydrofoil.

◁CHUNG SHAN HOT
SPRINGS, CHINA
The old and the new: a heavily
laden cyclist passes the
entrance to the club.

▽CLEARWATER BAY,
HONG KONG
The easiest way to reach this
course on a peninsula not far
from Hong Kong city is by
helicopter.

△CHUNG SHAN HOT
SPRINGS
A woman labours in the field
as golfers pass on the adjacent
fairway.

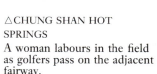

CHUNG SHAN HOT
SPRINGS▷
Arnold Palmer designed this
beautiful golf course, the first
new course in China. This is
the 9th hole, a par 4 which
requires an accurate second
shot.

◁CHUNG SHAN HOT
SPRINGS
Cheng Kwun Chi, the head
greens superintendent.

Japan consists of four main islands, and most of Japan's golf courses are built in hilly areas. They are designed to be enjoyed by all golfers, from beginners to professionals, with suitable undulations and the chance for strategic play.

Japanese people enjoy the seasonal changes throughout the year. It is especially wonderful to enjoy the glory of nature in each season. In spring, when the cherry and azalea are in full bloom, the golf course is remarkably beautiful. In summer, the greenery of the golf course reflected in the bright sunlight and the fragrance of new plants is very refreshing. Playing golf surrounded by the splendid tints of autumn is impressive. Even in winter, when the grass is dry, it's wonderful to be on the golf course in the fresh air, with snow-capped mountains clearly visible in the distance. In this way, golf in Japan can be enjoyed all year round.

Golf is becoming a more and more popular sport for Japanese people of all ages. It is also becoming a truly international sport, with more opportunities both for Japanese to play in other countries and for foreigners to play here. With its worldwide popularity, it would be a great thing if golf could unify all the peoples of the world.

TSUNEYUKI NAKAJIMA

KAWANA GOLF CLUB, JAPAN▷

NEW ST ANDREWS, TOKYO, JAPAN▷▷
The early morning mist rises from the valley beyond the short 8th hole.

JAPAN

ven the most seasoned golfing traveller cannot fail to be inspired by golf in the land of the rising sun.

At first sight the courses do not seem so dissimilar from hilly, undulating courses the world over, except that most will have two greens per hole, a bent grass green, and a rough-surfaced Korai green for use during the winter months. The two-green system will, however, be phased out in the next twenty-odd years, for the Japanese are now starting to follow the American example by using new strains of bent grass and mist systems to allow year-round play on the one surface.

By tradition your clubs will be carried or, more usually, pushed by a female caddie, who often takes charge of several bags simultaneously: indeed at some Japanese clubs electric trolleys run around the course on specially constructed underground rails, controlled automatically by your caddie. I am told that the tradition of women caddies began at Kawana, north of Tokyo, where the club boasts a seaside course not unlike Pebble Beach, and where caddying is done by the wives of fishermen from the local village. Bags are still carried individually at Kawana, and to this day each bag is weighed before play, and should it exceed a certain stipulated amount any surplus items are smartly removed.

Golf in Japan, for the fortunate few who enjoy access to a course, is an all-embracing experience, incorporating several important social rituals in addition to the game itself.

Most Japanese courses have the 9th green close to the clubhouse, so that players can enjoy not merely a snack or a noggin at the turn, but should they so desire, a full and leisurely meal. This means in practice that even the most enthusiastic devotee is hard pushed to play more than 27 holes in a day – indeed small refreshment huts dotted halfway around each nine emphasize that the basic rhythm of golf in Japan is of nine rather than eighteen holes.

At the conclusion of the day's play comes a major social occasion: the after-match bath. Every club has a fully equipped bath house, with separate facilities for men and women, and any resemblance between communal bathing Japanese-style and the traditional communal tub beloved of British football teams is purely accidental. In Japan it is customary to wash yourself thoroughly, sitting on a low wooden stool, below a shower unit mounted on the wall. Only when you are completely clean, with all traces of dirt and soap removed, do you enter the extremely hot communal bath, where the crucial golfing gossip of the day is exchanged.

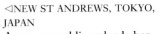NEW ST ANDREWS, TOKYO, JAPAN
A woman caddie unloads her electronically powered golf cart from the mono-rail which connects the two courses.

KAWANA, IZU, JAPAN▷
The par 5 13th hole of the Fuji Course, playing alongside the ocean. Similar to Pebble Beach in California, Kawana is Japan's top golf resort.

▽NASUNOGAHARA, TOKYO, JAPAN
A woman caddie makes tea halfway round the front nine.

Membership of a golf club in Japan is not something achieved by writing a polite letter to the club secretary and telephoning a few friends: it is something you discuss with your accountant, bank manager and indeed tax-lawyer!

Many club memberships in Japan are quoted on the Tokyo stock exchange, and can appreciate in value by up to 100 per cent per annum. Brokers now exist who trade solely in golf club memberships, just like any other share or commodity. Annual membership dues in 1987 ranged from a minimum of $20,000 to a top price of over $1.5 million: even then one cannot simply walk on to the first tee, as there is invariably a small monthly levy, and a considerable green fee to be paid prior to play. Club members have the choice of starting-times, and pay perhaps $40-$60 per day: non-members may pay up to $150 for a day's golf, if they can get a game at all.

It is common practice in Japan for golfers to take out an insurance against having a hole in one – for when that occurs it could cost them as much as a million yen. Not only would the unfortunate golfer buy drinks for his playing partners, as he would in most countries, he would also be expected to buy expensive presents for them, for the group in front, the group behind, and all the caddies, with a special gift for his own caddie. He would also probably plant a tree at the hole and maintain that tree for its (or his) lifetime.

The majority of serious golfers do manage to play perhaps once or twice a month in summer, but the cost and inconvenience are tremendous: there are over twenty companies in Tokyo alone specializing in the transport of golf equipment from the city to the course. Having made your reservation, travelled (at no small expense) out to the course, picked up your clubs from the carrier, you are then ready to play, perhaps two hours after starting out. The total cost of this exercise seems to Britons, or indeed North Americans, quite staggering, perhaps $250 a day. Small wonder that driving ranges are big business in Japan.

The image of thousands of avid Japanese golfers simultaneously driving balls into the floodlit night sky is a cherished one, but in fact many driving ranges are no bigger than half the size of a football pitch, with perhaps ten bays and a maximum shot length of 150 yards. Preventive nets, as much as 100 feet high, protect the public from aerial bombardment, and can be seen dotting the skyline of major cities. The biggest driving range in Japan is the Shiba, a three-storey semicircular construction with over 200 bays: this operates virtually twenty-four hours of the day and, like many Japanese driving ranges, has superb facilities.

Generalizations about 'national' characteristics are always dangerous, but it does seem that there is something in golf which accords with the Japanese psyche in a fundamental way – certainly the self-discipline, practice and constant effort required to succeed at the game are seen as

MAPLE COUNTRY CLUB,
MORIOKA, JAPAN
'Iwana's Long Hole', the 7th,
is so named because the grass
inside the bunker is shaped to
look like a fish, the *iwana* or
char.

△SHIBA DRIVING RANGE,
TOKYO, JAPAN

SHIBA DRIVING RANGE▷
The sun sets over Japan's
biggest driving range, with
hundreds of bays on three
levels. The area where the
balls land is designed so that
90 per cent of them return
automatically underground.

△SHIBA DRIVING RANGE,
TOKYO, JAPAN
Shiba is open for long hours
every day, and in the evening
business really starts to boom:
sometimes players may have
to wait up to three hours for
a space.

◁SHIBA DRIVING RANGE
The range even has a full-
sized teaching facility with a
proper bunker.

◁NEW ST ANDREWS, TOKYO, JAPAN
The 18th hole ready for floodlight play.

MARIYA, CHIBA, JAPAN▷
Mariya is the first golf course in Japan to be designed by Pete Dye. The 17th hole resembles the other dramatic island holes at TPC, Florida, and PGA West California.

MAPLE COUNTRY CLUB, MORIOKA, JAPAN▷▷
The 16th hole, called 'Hit and Pray', has a bunker in the shape of a maple leaf.

◁TOKYO
Two well-dressed girls walking along a Tokyo street on their way to a lunchtime practice session at a driving range.

△MAPLE COUNTRY CLUB,
MORIOKA, JAPAN
Caddies, old and new style.
At Maple Country Club a
uniformed caddie guides an
electronically powered trolley
carrying two sets of clubs,
while at New St Andrews the
remote control bag-carrying
cart rides along sensitized
tracks. At the traditional
Koganei, women still push the
clubs around.

KOGANEI, JAPAN▷

148

▽KOGANEI, JAPAN
An elderly maintenance worker tidies up a bunker.

distinct virtues, and there is little doubt that golf has now become an integral part of the lifestyle of many in Japan. Golf instruction is a small industry in its own right, and vast numbers of books, videos and cassettes are published every year: the mental side of golf, the famous 'Inner Game', is not neglected, and I once watched, fascinated, as the distinguished American golf teacher Dr Gary Wiren lectured to over two thousand Japanese businessmen on how they could apply themselves more effectively to practice and on how they could think themselves into improving their individual golf games.

Dr Wiren is one among dozens of visiting instructors who visit Japan each year, but of course the country now also has its own thriving professional tour. The exploits of Isao Aoki, who so nearly triumphed in the 1980 US Open at Baltusuol, only to be pipped at the last by Jack Nicklaus, have helped to focus the attention of the whole golfing world upon the extraordinary development of the game in the East. It can only be a matter of time before a Japanese player, perhaps Tommy Nakajima, takes one of golf's major championships.

The actual game in Japan represents in many ways a distinctive mixture of both North American and British influences, and yet it is nowadays quite wrong to think of golf solely as an imported phenomenon. One important recent development has been the emergence of Japanese-style golf complexes in other parts of the world, particularly where there are strong Japanese business interests. One such is the Old Thorns Country Club near Liphook in Hampshire, now owned and managed essentially for expatriate Japanese players, and in the USA there are several clubs with substantial Japanese membership: some addicts even fly in from Tokyo just for a Sunday game, which takes the traditional 'golfing weekend' into a wholly new dimension!

Japan itself desperately needs new courses, but the chronic over-crowding of the habitable islands means that competition for space is very considerable, and governments are naturally reluctant to sanction the conversion of scarce farmland into golf courses, despite the many employment opportunities such complexes provide. A limited amount of land has recently been given over to the game, but it seems likely that demand will always outstrip supply, and that many Japanese golfers will remain permanently starved of the real thing. The game nevertheless survives and prospers all over the country. Golf in Japan is alive and well.

NEW ST ANDREWS, TOKYO, JAPAN▷
Like its Scottish namesake, New St Andrews has a course named the Old Course
– complete with a bridge like the one over the Swilcan Burn (see page 38).

NASUNOGAHARA, JAPAN▷▷
A Japanese speciality: the golf bath. A thorough wash by the side of the pool is followed up with a soak in the tepid water and a review of the game just played.

Canada is such a vast country, but most of our golf courses are found in the southern part, due to the climate. There is such a variety of areas and courses, from the links course of the Victoria Golf Club to the far reaches of Prince Edward Island and Newfoundland. Where else can you play in the shadow of such natural beauty as the Canadian Rockies? And through the central prairies we find numerous golf courses surrounded by the grandeur of National Parks.

Many courses of tremendous calibre can be found in our metropolitan areas. Notably, Glen Abbey in Toronto, home of the Canadian Open, where each year PGA golfers compete for Canada's national championship. The Royal Montreal and the Royal Quebec are two of the oldest clubs in North America.

Towards Eastern Canada you will find the beauty of the lakes and streams that make up some of the finest golf anywhere. In the east-coast villages you can play a round of golf under beautiful sunshine and dine at the 19th hole on fresh lobster.

Canada's Professional Golf Tour has attracted players from around the world. The circuit takes them through seven of Canada's ten provinces. For something different you could enter a Midnight Tournament in the Yukon. That's right, with twenty-four hours of sunlight in the summer a tee time could be midnight.

I hope when golf and beauty enter your mind, you will think of Canada.

DAN HALLDORSON

GLEN ABBEY, CANADA▷

CANADA

Golf in Canada is a very different game from the one played only a few miles from its southern border in the United States. While many facets of the American game have infiltrated golf here, it is still true to say that golf in Canada is closer to the game played in the British Isles than in the USA.

Perhaps because it is further north, and temperatures are therefore more moderate, walking a golf course in Canada, even in the heat of the summer, is not as uncommon as it is in America. While many Canadian clubs do have golf carts, many people still walk.

Canada is a vast and varied country and golf is played on all sorts of terrain, from the east to the west coast. Toronto, with over a hundred golf courses within fairly easy reach of the city, has one of the biggest golfing populations of any city in North America, and all the big cities in Canada are well endowed with golfing facilities.

With so many courses of such high calibre it is hard to know which to pick out for special mention. Not only are most of the courses old and well established, but many have been designed by famous golf architects. One of the greatest Canadian architects was Stanley Thompson, who designed, among others, the Banff Springs course set in the rugged Canadian Rockies (see pages 160-161). Thompson was born in Scotland but spent most of his life in Vancouver. There he designed perhaps his best course, Capilano, set against a backdrop of mountains with a magnificent view overlooking Vancouver harbour.

Golf in Canada can be a little more pricey than it is south of the border. First, land costs in general are high, and secondly the golf clubs that are built tend to be exclusively for golf. The resorts, however, are generally not as crowded as those in, say, Florida, and therefore their rates are more competitive.

Canada is, to my mind, one of the best places in the world to play golf. The climate from April to October is ideal. The Canadians have taken the best from their neighbours in the south and combined it with the finest traditions of the game. The result is a blend unique to their country.

△NATIONAL GOLF CLUB,
TORONTO, CANADA
The 17th hole, with the 18th
heading up the hill on the left.
The perfect conditioning here
sets a standard that all courses
strive to attain.

BANFF SPRINGS, ALBERTA,
CANADA▷
The final hole at Banff
Springs, one of the most
beautiful settings anywhere in
the world for a golf course.

159

Golf in South America had its beginnings in Argentina, later spreading to Chile, Colombia and eventually to all of Latin America. Towards the end of the last century, the British who had migrated to Argentina began to build the railroads in that country. To encourage the movement of the population away from the crowded centre to the outskirts of Buenos Aires, the golf-loving English built a few courses.

For a long time the number of courses could be counted on the fingers of one hand, but they increased along with the population growth. Argentina, with 200 courses, continues as the leader in South America. Buenos Aires has two municipal courses as well as driving ranges that are open to the public; Bogota, Colombia, has one public course; all the others, in the various countries, are private clubs.

South American golf course architects regularly go to the United States to study modern methods, so that recently constructed courses follow international lines with such features as dogleg fairways and undulating greens.

All the countries now have professional and amateur golf associations, competing in important international tournaments like the World Cup, as well as within their own borders. A number of pros have emerged who have gained international recognition.

We remain hopeful that, given time and a more favourable financial climate in Latin America, we will be able to attract a greater number of players to this wonderful game which plays such an important role in the lives of those who get to know it.

ROBERTO DE VICENZO

CASA DE CAMPO, DOMINICAN REPUBLIC▷

LATIN AMERICA

△LA PAZ, BOLIVIA
The drive to the club is almost as spectacular as the golf course itself.

△LA PAZ
A woman sells beer in the main street of Bolivia; perhaps she would have done better with sales on the golf course.

LA PAZ▷
A dramatic tee on the par 3 12th hole which plays over these stalagmite-like rocks to a small green. As it is the highest golf course in the world, the air is thin and the ball carries easily.

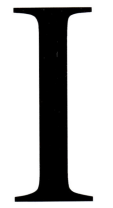

In compiling this section I have decided to include not only the South American continent itself, but also the outlying islands and states of Central America.

In general, Latin American golf presents a distinctive blend of features from both Europe and the USA, and nowhere is this more striking than in Argentina, probably the major centre of the game in South America. For many years a visit to Argentina was *de rigueur* for nomadic professionals, and back in the 1920s the young Henry Cotton spent a winter season at the palatial Mar del Plata club outside Buenos Aires. Argentina itself has a fine tradition of producing good golfers, and dominated the early years of the World Cup (then called the Canada Cup), winning the inaugural event in 1953. Roberto De Vicenzo is unquestionably the finest player to have emerged from Argentina, and it is doubly unfortunate that to many people he will always be remembered for an event he tragically lost, the Masters of 1968, after signing an incorrect card, rather than for the Open Championship which he in fact won, at Hoylake in 1967.

South America boasts not only two of the highest golf courses in the world, at Tuctu in Peru and La Paz, Bolivia, but also one of the most southerly, at the foot of Argentina. Not surprisingly golf in South America is played on terrain of tremendous variety, as the photographs demonstrate.

Golf clubs in South America are basically of two types; there are the old-established institutions, founded and still controlled by the indigenous upper-classes, as well as a growing number of resort complexes on the North American model, found particularly on the Mexican coast, in the Caribbean, and in Brazil. Such resorts are equipped with all the facilities a visiting American golfer would expect, and some of the courses are quite outstanding, notably Pete Dye's masterpiece at Casa de Campo in the Dominican Republic.

Built under the auspices of the Gulf and Western oil company, Casa de Campo has eight holes not so much beside the sea as in it: many of the trees and greens are almost totally surrounded by water, and the azure blue of the Caribbean with its foaming white surf and the lush velvety fairways make a matchless spectacle. The resident chairman of Gulf and Western built a luxury home for himself on a prime spot overlooking the ocean, and the resort itself is of an equivalent standard. When the 'artists' village' on top of the neighbouring hill was finished, complete with a stone amphitheatre modelled on the Colosseum in Rome, Frank Sinatra and his ensemble were flown in especially for the opening ceremony. As you can see, there is nothing understated about Casa de Campo.

THE JOCKEY CLUB, BUENOS AIRES▷
Looking across to the 2nd hole of this magnificent Mackenzie-designed course.

Within the West Indies, Jamaica is a justly popular holiday destination, although its many splendid courses have not received quite the same lavish treatment as elsewhere in the Caribbean. Players are still permitted, indeed encouraged, to walk, rather than use the ubiquitous carts, and Half Moon Bay and Tryall in particular offer a spectacular blend of great golf and beautiful scenery.

One of the most reassuring things about golf the world over is the way that many clubs and courses seem to survive external political crises almost untouched. With the possible exception of Africa, no other part of the world has suffered quite such continuous political turbulence in recent times as South America, yet the game of golf has survived and prospered. During the great period of nationalist upheaval in the late nineteenth century, strong trading links meant that many visiting Britons helped to found and develop golf clubs in Argentina, and this tradition has continued into the present century, with America now leading the way.

A bag of golf clubs can prove more effective than any passport, as I once discovered for myself. Trying to enter a nameless South American republic, I had all my extremely valuable photographic equipment impounded at the airport customs. For a while disaster loomed, as my party could go neither out nor in, and seemed totally stranded. Yet one phone call to our prospective host golf club, and within hours we (and our precious equipment) were free to move on.

Golf in South America still remains, by and large, the preserve of the rich and powerful, and the sense of brotherhood among golfers is strong. That said, geographical and political considerations probably make any kind of South American professional 'tour', on the American or European model, impractical, although each country has its own national championships, some of which are of great antiquity. Indeed the Argentinian Amateur, founded in 1895, is the fifth oldest such championship in the world.

The climate and terrain of the continent do mean that golf in South America tends to be a sport for the reasonably fit and energetic. In the tropical regions of Chile very high temperatures discourage the game during summer, yet in winter it is possible to ski in the morning, play golf in the afternoon, and without travelling any great distance, swim in the sea in the evening! Only North California and New Zealand can provide an equivalent range of contrasting sporting facilities within such a small area.

Perhaps my abiding memory of golf in South America, and a powerful example of the joy it can bring, was in Bolivia, one of the poorest and most strife-torn countries in the continent, with an annual rate of inflation in excess of 120 per cent. Martial law is commonplace, and when I passed through it looked as if the capital La Paz was virtually under

△HALF MOON BAY CLUB,
JAMAICA
A view across the lily pond to
the 16th hole (right) and the
ocean in the distance.

TRYALL GOLF CLUB,
HANOVER, JAMAICA▷
Jamaica in all its glory: the
flowers, the tropical landscape
and the Caribbean coastline
– and, to complete the picture,
a challenging golf course.

◁TRYALL GOLF CLUB
The 3rd green and the 4th tee
could hardly be closer to the
warm and inviting Caribbean.

169

ROSE HALL GOLF CLUB,
TRYALL, JAMAICA▷
A colourful Jamaican caddie.

CASA DE CAMPO, DOMINICAN
REPUBLIC▷
Caddies practise on their own
improvised course in the back
yard behind the professionals'
shop.

172

△CASA DE CAMPO,
DOMINICAN REPUBLIC
A greenskeeper proudly helps
to keep this ocean-side course
in the condition that attracts
players from all over the world.

◁CASA DE CAMPO
Caddies and greenskeepers
gather stones to help reinforce
the tees built in the breakwater
which are continually battered
by the waves.

△THE JOCKEY CLUB,
BUENOS AIRES
The substantial stone
clubhouse looks more like a
Tudor mansion, and would do
credit to any old-established
club in Europe.

◁THE JOCKEY CLUB
The 3rd hole is a par 3
elevated green with beautifully
sculpted bunkers cutting deep
into the front and side of the
green. The hole is surrounded
by trees of all shapes and sizes.

siege. Yet up at the golf club everything was very different. Parties of singing and dancing golfers were celebrating the end of a good day out on the course as if there was no tomorrow.

In such countries it is often a struggle for golf clubs to survive, but the game creates such tangible warmth and goodwill among people of all creeds, colours and classes that survive it does. All in all, few parts of the world seem to offer as much pleasure from the simple act of hitting a golf ball as South America.

World-rated golfers from South America have been few and far between. But who can dispute the enormous contribution made to the game by such diverse but distinguished players as Roberto De Vicenzo, Chi Chi Rodriguez and Lee Trevino. These legends overcame poverty, the lack of facilities, courses and tuition to establish themselves as household names.

The existing deprivation and the meagre development of golf courses on this turbulent continent severely restrict the opportunities for players to emerge, and this, in my opinion, is a tragedy for golf. For the above triumvirate share one quality – charisma – which is largely missing from today's tour stars.

Roberto De Vicenzo, big, bluff and handsome, was one of the pioneers of golf in South America. His enormous strength, allied to a wonderful touch, enabled him to capture numerous titles worldwide – including the British Open. Today he is but an infrequent visitor to the US Seniors' Tour, but when the spirit moves him he is as gifted as any of his peers.

That Seniors' Tour is dominated by Chi Chi Rodriguez. In 1987 the slim, wise-cracking Puerto Rican won seven events and amassed more than $500,000. He has been a regular in the US since 1960. His abiding philosophy has been that of a man who went from rags to riches but never forgot his origins. A committed anti-drugs campaigner, Chi Chi has helped raise vast sums for charity and many a laugh along the way.

Trevino – Supermex, Superstar, Superguy, call him what you will – is arguably the most gifted player in the history of golf, and certainly the funniest. He needs no testimonial from me. Suffice to say that whenever I approach him on golf business, I couldn't meet a more helpful person. Lee learned his golf by playing with a taped-up Coke bottle, and progressed through the caddie ranks to become the most popular figure in global golf. Like Chi Chi, he has had a few bumps along the road, but he too has always remembered how it all began. For instance, when he won the British Open at Royal Birkdale for the first time, he gave away his winner's cheque to a local convent in Southport, Lancashire. Latterly, Trevino has taken to TV commentary work like a Mexican to tequila. No matter in what sphere, he will remain an inspiration to those Latin golfers who also aspire to greater things.

CASA DE CAMPO, DOMINICAN REPUBLIC▷
The 5th green provides a small target with no room for error on any side.
GAVEA, RIO DE JANEIRO▷▷
Even when the sun doesn't shine, the golfers who are lucky enough to play here have a unique setting, with the beach on one side and mountains rising steeply on the other.

Most American golfers who play Britain's great links courses on vacation trips thoroughly enjoy the experience. Give them comparable conditions as a steady diet back home and I think the majority of them would throw a fit. The reason is that, once its novelty has worn off, golf-as-it-was-in-the-beginning simply doesn't supply what they have come to seek from the game.

In both work and play Americans expect the payoff to match the input. If they do a lousy job – in an office or on a golf course – they'll accept the unpleasant consequences, but if they do a good one they demand a proportionate reward. Roller-coaster fairways, cement-like greens and thigh-high rough may be okay for a brief change of pace, but as permanent fixtures they raise golf's luck factor way too high for most Yankees. We tend quickly to reach a point where watching a well-planned, perfectly struck approach shot kick sideways off an invisible hummock and bury itself in a bunker just isn't what we are paying our money for.

Compounding this mind-set is our preoccupation with numbers as a means of measuring how well or badly we do at sports. This translates in golf into wanting to 'shoot a number' almost as much as wanting to win. Even when we compete head to head, most of us still tend to *think* in stroke play terms, which makes overall scores a lot more important to us than to golfers in countries where the match result is what matters most.

Another factor behind the large amounts of money, sweat and love that go into American course conditioning is the US climate. A dry spell in Scotland turns all that fine indigenous fescue light brown and dead-looking, but it reverts to a healthy green the moment the rains return. In many parts of our country – the huge desert regions, for instance – there would be no grass at all without constant heavy feeding and watering.

I mention these factors just to offer a little more perspective to Brian's fine portrayal – both pictorially and verbally – of golf American-style. I'm personally very proud that my country makes such a distinctive contribution.

JACK NICKLAUS

United States of America

△MORNINGSIDE, CALIFORNIA, USA

AUGUSTA NATIONAL, GEORGIA, USA▷
An early scene on the 15th hole at Augusta National. The bridge in the background has been named after Gene Sarazen to commemorate his famous shot here.

olf in the USA is as diverse as the fifty states themselves. The image conjured up each year by television and magazine coverage of the three American major championships suggests that all American golf is played on lush, manicured courses resplendent with acres of white sand and numerous water-hazards.

Beautiful and spectacular golf courses there certainly are, often constructed out of the most unpromising terrain and with annual budgets for maintenance and upkeep that would be unbelievable anywhere else. Many of the larger clubs spend over $1 million a year on keeping their facilities in trim, and it is not surprising that at almost every country club monthly membership dues exceed $150, on top of an initial entry fee of perhaps $15,000-plus. Some prospective members may even be required to invest in club property, a financial commitment that may run into millions of dollars. At some of the top resort courses the fees for a single round exceed the cost of a whole year's golf in Britain.

Arriving for his or her first game in the USA, a visitor from overseas will first of all be struck by the rigorous security. Unlike Britain and much of the rest of the world, where visiting golfers are generally made welcome except at particularly busy times, in America it is often impossible to play at a private club unless accompanied by a member. At many such clubs, golf is in any case only one among many sporting and social activities on offer. Country clubs seem to expand every year, as swimming pools, tennis courts, saunas and jacuzzi baths are added in profusion. Active golfers may well be in a minority, but the whole complex will be kept in tip-top condition, partly of course out of a wish to emulate such fabulous creations as Augusta National, almost certainly the best groomed golf course in the world.

Augusta certainly sets the standard that the rest of America tries to follow, and across the country greenskeepers have watered, mown, fertilized and done absolutely everything in their power to convert their home patch into something similar. If truth be told this has not always been successful, and the actual playability of several once-distinguished golf courses has been badly damaged. Many of the older courses were designed to accommodate a bump-and-run type shot, and were at their most challenging when the fairways were burnt dry. The great courses designed by Donald Ross at Pinehurst and elsewhere exemplified this, with lethally fast, elevated greens, strategic fairway bunkers, but little directly in front of the putting surface to prevent the straight shot from pitching short and running up to the pin. In very dry spells this was often the only way to play the hole. However, the universal desire to 'green up' golf courses has caused such shots to become almost redundant, and

PINEHURST, NORTH CAROLINA, USA▷
Pinehurst became the home of the father of golf-course architecture, Donald Ross. He lavished much attention on this, the best known of his courses, the No. 2.

LA QUINTA, CALIFORNIA, USA▷ ▷
The rising sun brings the desert to life on this mountain course in Palm Springs.

184

over-watering means that soft, almost puddingy greens will hold practically anything hit to them. Careful positioning of the drive becomes almost irrelevant, as the second shot can now be hit from almost any angle and still hold the green. Some would argue that a lot of the tactical, head-scratching aspect of the game has disappeared, and that is perhaps why many American golfers are now coming to Britain, to places like Dornoch and Ballybunion, to savour seaside golf at its most natural and primitive.

If much of the game in America is effectively target golf, there nevertheless exists a great variety of courses, each the product of differing soils and climate. In the wetlands of Florida, huge ponds have been dug out of the flat terrain, and the earth used to create raised tees and greens and provide some relief in the otherwise rather flat, uninspiring landscape. In the northern states of New England, Oregon and Washington, conditions are not unlike those in Britain, and some of the older layouts could easily be mistaken for Wentworth or one of the Surrey heather-and-pine courses. In high upland areas such as Denver, Colorado, scene of Arnold Palmer's famous US Open win in 1960, courses have to be lengthened by perhaps 10 per cent beyond the norm, simply to accommodate the extra distances the ball can be hit through the thin mountain air.

Despite its huge stretch of coastline, America has curiously few seaside links, in the true sense of the word. Ben Hogan's favourite course in the whole country, Seminole in Florida, is a wonderful exception, and Maidstone on Long Island has a few links holes, but traditional linksland in the Scottish manner scarcely exists. The warm climate encourages rapid and verdant growth, and in any case much of the American golfing public is rather suspicious of such 'bounce golf', as it is sometimes rudely called. Pebble Beach itself is a public course by the sea, but is essentially a cliff-top rather than duneland layout, and its near-neighbours Spyglass Hill and Cypress Point both contain holes rather closer to the original links ideal. Cypress Point, with its famous 15th and 16th holes across the Pacific, is perhaps the most beautifully varied golf course in the world, taking in at least three distinct types of terrain in the course of eighteen holes.

Cypress is also highly unusual in that it is a golf club pure and simple, and players on foot are still encouraged. I have heard it said, in all seriousness, that electric carts have given American golf a totally new lease of life, and certainly millions of older people have been attracted to the game who would otherwise have been physically incapable of walking five or six miles at a stretch. There are apparently seventeen million people playing at least seven rounds of golf a year in the USA, and I would guess that the great majority, perhaps 75 per cent, have never walked a complete course. Many courses do not allow walkers and insist

THE HONORS COURSE, CHATTANOOGA, TENNESSEE, USA▷
A view from behind the par 4 9th hole.

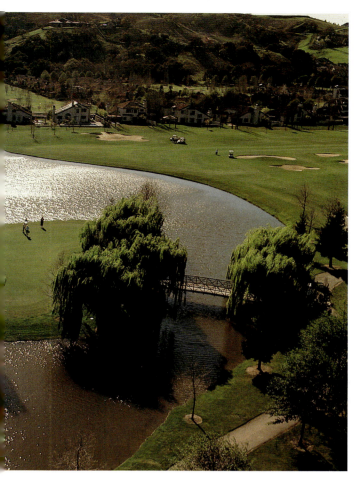

◁CASTLE PINES, COLORADO, USA

◁◁BLACKHAWK, CALIFORNIA, USA

◁◁◁AUGUSTA NATIONAL, GEORGIA, USA

Clubhouses in America, as in other countries, often reflect the architecture of the area. Augusta National transformed an old plantation building while Shinnecock Hills hired Stanford White to design theirs. Modern clubs such as Castle Pines and Morning-side spent millions on architecturally exciting and memorable buildings, whereas resorts such as Blackhawk have simply aimed to make theirs fit in with the residential environment.

◁MORNINGSIDE, CALIFORNIA, USA

◁◁SHINNECOCK HILLS, LONG ISLAND, NEW YORK, USA

MAIDSTONE, NEW YORK, USA▷

The par 3 8th hole situated in the middle of the linksland is one of the few places in the United States where pure links golf can be played. The holes along the ocean here are reminiscent of those found on similar land in Britain.

on players taking a cart and once, when visiting the PGA National Complex in Florida, my daughter was informed that she could not even walk behind our game, but would have to hire a separate cart if she wanted to follow us around.

To the hardy British golfer this may seem almost farcical, but you cannot fail to be struck by the sheer scale of the golf-cart operation. At the major American resorts, with perhaps a handful of courses attached, it is not uncommon to find parking spaces for up to 2000 carts, each of which has to be cleaned and recharged every day. As these carts can cost up to $15,000 each, affluent private owners often build a separate berth in which to house their precious status symbols, adjacent to their orthodox garages. Golf cart 'extras' range from a drinks cooler and ventilation fan to television and radio, so that avid sports fans can keep up with the latest football and baseball news whilst out on the course. Some carts are styled like Rolls-Royces, some like Jaguars, and others are completely personalized according to the whim of the owner. Bob Hope owns a cart shaped after his own profile, complete with huge nose!

In spite of the onset of automation, human caddies still survive, and again the example of Augusta has been influential. Several clubs now insist on at least one caddie per couple, sometimes in addition to the standard electric cart. The white-overalled caddie will drive the cart where necessary, staying on the designated cart path, whilst the golfers walk on in front, swapping with the caddie whenever there's a long walk to the next tee. At many of the older clubs, like historic Inverness in Toledo, Ohio, long-established caddie programmes exist, utilizing keen students and others in search of summer employment. The older full-time caddies often spend the summer months in the northern states and then follow the migrant golfers south for the winter, to one of the luxury resort complexes in Florida or southern California.

There is an abundance of such resorts throughout America, from the mountains of Colorado to the shores of South Carolina, and from the Arizona desert to the hills of West Virginia. Each tries to outdo its rivals with increasingly elaborate facilities, superbly kept courses and the best available tuition, and they naturally vie with each other to hire the finest teachers in the profession. Players arrive in droves every week, expecting to find some miracle cure for their particular golfing ailments, and are prepared to undergo the most extraordinary and uncomfortable treatment to achieve this. The more sophisticated, expensive and outlandish the teaching method, the more popular it seems to be. I have seen everything, from weird mechanical contraptions that hold the various parts of the body in the correct position, to a computerized video aid which analyses the swings of the top tour professionals and then assesses the extent to which your own swing fits, or distorts, this approved pattern.

GRAND CYPRESS, FLORIDA, USA▷
The 16th hole, designed by Jack Nicklaus, who managed to re-create a bit of Scotland on a piece of flat ground in Florida.

DESERT HIGHLANDS, ARIZONA, USA▷▷
The magnificent par 5 2nd hole: three islands of greenery in the middle of the natural desert, surrounded by enormous saworo cacti – some grow as high as twenty-five feet.

CHERRY HILLS GOLF CLUB, COLORADO, USA▷

There are plenty of animals to be seen around golf courses in America. Pictured here are swans at Cherry Hills in Denver, a rattlesnake at La Paloma, Tucson, an alligator at Seabrook on Hilton Head Island, and a deer on the course at Merion. And at Disney Wee Links, the mini course for children in Florida, Donald Duck flies the flag.

SEABROOK, SOUTH CAROLINA, USA▷

△LA PALOMA, ARIZONA, USA

△ MERION GOLF CLUB,
PENNSYLVANIA, USA

◁DISNEY WEE LINKS,
FLORIDA, USA

199

One feature of golf at many such resorts that may seem rather strange to the British visitor is the relaxed attitude to the rules. Of course in properly organized competitions the rules are strictly adhered to, but in ordinary casual games it is not unusual, for example, to permit yourself a second drive from the first tee, commonly known as a 'mulligan'. Many occasional players tend to regard the basic rule of golf, that the ball must be played where it lies, as at best a general principle, rather than an absolute law. Lies are constantly 'preferred', even in the height of summer, causing intense annoyance to the serious player, who regards this 'f-l-o-g' as a total inversion of the true spirit of the game of golf.

Golf in America is very largely a four-ball game: the classic, alternate-shot 'Scotch' foursome probably only arises in the country once every couple of years, during the Walker or Ryder Cup matches. The permutations devised to vary this staple four-ball diet are tremendous, and one particularly combative and enjoyable form of the game takes place at Arnold Palmer's home club. There the regular daily shoot-out consists of one professional, one good amateur, and two others of middling ability. Both the best and the next-best balls count, and interest in the game is always maintained for everyone. 'Scramble' is another popular format, and I have played it in several American Pro-Am competitions. In Scramble everyone tees off, and then all four players hit their second shots from where the best drive finishes. This is then repeated on the green, and again all four players putt from the position of the nearest approach to the pin. Everyone is 'in at the death', and the weaker players need never feel left out. Golfers throughout the world are constantly inventing new forms of the game, but the Americans still seem far and away the most inventive.

I suppose if I had to make one criticism of golf in the USA today, it would be the simple fact that so few people appreciate the joys of walking round the course. Too much capital has been invested in electric carts, by clubs, professionals and amateurs alike, for there ever to be a fundamental reversal of the present trend, but one encouraging recent development must be the advent of the motorized pull-cart, which provides the best of both worlds. It would be nice to think that this will enable golfers no longer in the first flush of youth to carry on playing the game, and still obtain much-needed exercise from walking eighteen holes. Such pull-carts might also speed things up a little. Given time, a day's golf in the USA might once again come to mean 36 holes – even perhaps with 'another nine after tea'! I certainly hope so. American golf is one of the great glories of the game, and every player should try and sample its contrasting delights at first hand.

Arnold Palmer is generally credited with shooting golf from the nickel

COUNTRY CLUB OF THE ROCKIES, COLORADO, USA▷
The par 5 17th hole near the ski resorts in Vail, where golf is fast becoming the way to fill up empty hotels in the summer. This new course has been joined by five others, all built within the last few years.

LAKE NONA, FLORIDA, USA▷▷
The bunker comes into play for more than half of the 18th hole as the cypress trees seem to grow out of the water.

△SPYGLASS HILL,
CALIFORNIA, USA

An unusual sight in America, where most people ride electric golf carts: two players walking up the hill on the 2nd hole.

PGA TOUR PRACTICE GROUND▷

Practice grounds are normally busy places, but never more than when Tour golfers hit town.

◁THE HONORS COURSE,
CHATTANOOGA,
TENNESSEE, USA
Augusta is one of the few
courses still to have white-
suited caddies – a tradition
continued here at
Chattanooga.

OLYMPIC CLUB, SAN
FRANCISCO, USA▷
This shot of the uphill 18th
hole at sunrise shows off the
extraordinary beauty of this
part of northern California.

▽INVERNESS, OHIO, USA
A proud caddie-master shows
off his caddie crew for the
summer. This course in
Toledo has one of the best
caddie programmes in the
United States.

and dime into a multi-billion-dollar industry. Even now, in the twilight of a unique career, Arnie still commands an army wherever he plays. The handsome Palmer had a love affair with the camera lens. The familiar hitch of his trousers, flat-to-the-boards swing and win-or-bust approach were ready-made for a rapidly expanding television industry. Arnie was shortly joined by tenacious South African Gary Player and a crew-cut youngster called Jack Nicklaus, and golf's Holy Trinity was formed.

The Big Three, given unprecedented exposure through the medium of television, converted millions of new fans to the game. They also brought millions of dollars to each of their bank accounts. The money-making process was boosted and skilfully manipulated by a Cleveland accountant, Mark McCormack. Now head of the powerful IMG organization, McCormack's expertise and entrepreneurial flair fired industry with a desire to become involved in the game of golf. Sponsorship deals were signed, endorsements tied up, coffers prised open and money flowed into golf as never before.

While many were envious of the status of the Big Three, and judging by their tour records at that time in the 1960s not without some justification, the benefits to golf overall were staggering. Professional golf soared into the big league and has continued to grow ever since.

In 1987, Floridian Paul Azinger won $822,481. How much of that was made possible by Palmer's buccaneering ways? While today's leading protagonists are all millionaires, enjoying a lifestyle and fame they once only dreamed of, the Big Three have not fared badly either.

Palmer pilots his own jet, has an annual income he can't count, designs a few courses, owns property in Latrobe, Pennsylvania, and Bay Hill, Florida. At the latter he also owns Bay Hill GC which hosts the annual Bay Hill Classic on the US Tour. He is the eternal favourite of galleries throughout the world, irrespective of his fading talents.

Player is still highly competitive and a potent force on the Seniors' Tour. He is a living example of the maxim: practice makes perfect. A devoted family man, he relaxes on his huge ranch in South Africa where he breeds thoroughbred racehorses and raises cattle.

Nicklaus, with career earnings of $5 million, is the greatest and most successful golfer in the history of the game. With seventy-one wins to his credit, the Golden Bear's place in the Hall of Fame is assured. But Jack will also be remembered as one of the most distinctive, creative golf architects ever.

At the other end of the golfing scale, some of tomorrow's would-be stars still have to sacrifice for success. Some buy Motor Homes and, with their families, follow a precarious existence in the shadow of the tour. Others form cliques, share transport and cheap hotel rooms to minimize costs in their pursuit of fame and fortune. It is not uncommon for

SPYGLASS HILL, CALIFORNIA, USA▷
The pampas grass waves gently in the breeze and the natural sand-dunes make an idyllic setting for this, the 5th hole.

◁MUIRFIELD VILLAGE, OHIO, USA
The Memorial Garden at Jack Nicklaus's club in Dublin, Ohio. Every year a player is honoured during the tournament, and has a bronze placed in the Memorial Garden. Shown here is the bronze of Gene Sarazen.

△WATERWAY HILLS, SOUTH CAROLINA, USA
A chairlift is used to transport golfers over a river to this course at Myrtle Beach.

PGA WEST STADIUM COURSE, CALIFORNIA, USA▷
The 17th hole was created by Pete Dye, echoing the one he first built on the TPC course in Jacksonville, Florida.

△LOS COLINAS, TEXAS, USA
A typical resort hotel, with the golf carts parked around the Star of Texas ready for the day's play.

◁PGA WEST STADIUM COURSE, CALIFORNIA, USA
The golf carts in Palm Springs have everything from ice boxes to televisions. They even have radiator grilles in the Rolls-Royce style, but are called Royal Rides.

OAKLAND HILLS, MICHIGAN, USA▷
As the early morning mist rises from the fairway it reveals the immaculate conditioning of the course.

struggling pros to drive from Los Angeles to Florida for the next event.

Today's all-exempt tour has many critics. It is argued that it has produced a generation of golfing clones; that it has helped tilt the balance of golfing power to Britain and Europe. The feats of Seve Ballesteros, Greg Norman and Bernhard Langer substantiate that argument. Yet the US Tour, which proliferates each year, still remains the toughest place in the world to earn a living.

MISSION HILLS, CALIFORNIA, USA▷
The 18th hole, with its island green a par 5, looks almost too good to be true. The course is real – only the swans are plastic.

△ELK RIVER, NORTH CAROLINA, USA
The 16th hole, bounded by a stream, is a difficult target, especially with the deep bunker on the front right of the green.

▽OAK TREE, OKLAHOMA, USA
The 16th hole has a hangman's rope on a tree nearby. Obviously if you take too many shots here you have a get-out.

△AUGUSTA NATIONAL,
GEORGIA, USA
Amen Corner got its name
from the three pivotal holes
on the back nine. The middle
hole in that group is the
majestic par 3 12th hole which
plays over Rae's Creek.

PEBBLE BEACH, CALIFORNIA,
USA▷
One of the best finishing holes
in golf: the par 5 18th hole,
with the sun rising over the
hills. It is the tree which makes
the third shot – or the second,
if you are brave – so difficult.

◁DISNEY WEE LINKS,
FLORIDA, USA
At this course specially built
for children to learn to play,
the tees are of astroturf and
the greens are artificial, so that
even the wildest of youngsters
cannot do much damage.

Index of Golf Courses

◁BONITA BAY, FLORIDA, USA
A bird's eye view of the golf course at Bonita Bay.

Africa, India and the Arab States

Figures in *italic* refer to illustrations.

◁PRINCEVILLE, HAWAII, USA
The dramatic par 3 16th hole, with the island of Bali in the background.

AUSTRALIA, NEW ZEALAND AND THE FAR EAST

CANADA

EUROPE

GREAT BRITAIN AND IRELAND

JAPAN